M000286157

May this book help you find
greater joy along your journey
in life + love!

Les + Susan Parrott

ENJOY
the Journey
Along Your
MARRIAGE HIGHWAY

Nurture Joy Forever
with the
6 Practices for
Thriving Relationships

W. C. "Tres" Tanner III, Ph.D.
and
Susan Tanner, M.S.

Copyright © 1997 by W. C. Tanner III & Susan T. Tanner
All rights reserved. No part of this book may be reproduced or transmitted, in any form or by any means, without permission in writing from the publisher, except in the case of brief quotations in critical reviews and certain other noncommercial uses permitted by copyright law.

This book is available in quantity discounts for educational, counseling, business, or sales promotional use. For further information on bulk sales or permission requests, contact the publisher at:

HOME/WORK®—The Family Connection®
15721 Bernardo Heights Parkway, Suite E-410
San Diego, CA 92128
Phone: Toll Free 1-888-3HOMEWORK (1-888-346-6396)
Fax: (619) 675-7504

First Edition: August 1997

Editorial/Design/Production:
Executive Excellence Publishing
1344 East 1120 South
Provo, Utah 84606
(801) 375-4060

10 9 8 7 6 5 4 3 2 1   02 01 00 99 98 97

ISBN Number: 1-890009-25-3

Cover Design by Ginger McGovern

Printed in the United States of America by Publishers Press

We dedicate this book to each other.

Each of us is deeply grateful in ways that words cannot describe for how our lives have been abundantly blessed since finding each other.

We cannot begin to express our thankfulness for the privilege of being married to:

a chosen companion to share life with,

a wife/husband we care for as our best friend,

a soulmate we love to connect with,

a spouse we can confront about "tough stuff,"

a helpmate to resolve our challenges with,

a life partner to grow with forever.

We appreciate the privilege of relishing life and experiencing joy—together!

ACKNOWLEDGMENTS

$\mathscr{T}RES$: I appreciate the thousands of clients, students, and seminar participants who have given me opportunities to help them experience greater joy in their families. Much of my understanding about couples has come as they bared their souls in my counseling office, carried out learning assignments in college courses, and shared personal insights during the interactive learning experiences of professional seminars. I'm also grateful for the knowledge and insights gleaned from many professors, authors, and professional colleagues. Their individual and collective contributions to my understanding could never be fully explained here.

Most of all, I'm thankful for Susan. She has brought so much love into my life. I'm grateful for her belief in me and her incredibly patient support of me. At a deep and personal level, she has restored my appreciation of how wonderful marriage can be—and thus my motivation to undertake this project. It was her idea that we write this book; her zealous persistence has kept us forging forward to complete the task. Some of the differences between us have proven invaluable in our collaborative effort as writers. Her ability to express ideas simply, concisely, and in practical ways is reflected throughout the book.

$\mathscr{S}USAN$: I greatly appreciate my wonderful husband, Tres, for his commitment to helping families, and especially couples, who are the heart of the family. I am also most appreciative to our children for their tolerance, patience, and support during these months that we've been so intensely focused on writing this book.

RES AND SUSAN: We are particularly indebted to our outstanding support team at Executive Excellence. We never could have carried out this project without the functions they fulfilled as our editors and literary agents. Moreover, their direction, feedback, encouragement, and patience were crucial. Of special note, we'd like to mention Ken Shelton for his vision in appreciating its potential, his incisive recommendations, and his overall leadership in orchestrating all of the editorial and literary agent functions of his staff. Especially in this regard we thank Trent Price and Jennifer Smith for their extensive editorial help with the various versions of the manuscript, and for their craft in helping with the layout, graphics, and other aspects of the project. We also thank Ginger McGovern for her work on the cover design as well as the artful text layout and graphics in the book. We also appreciate the assistance of Michael Russell, Heman Smith, and Richard Allen for their valuable contributions in marketing and promoting the book and our work and programs. The entire staff at Executive Excellence Publishing has been most cooperative in accommodating our visits and telephone calls, and in working with us in general under rather challenging circumstances.

We feel our book is much better because of the extensive computer graphic design support provided by Quent Wells and the wonderful illustration by George Thomas. Much thanks to both of you.

Our special thanks to those who took the time to review earlier versions of the manuscript and give us their valuable feedback: Those who shared their perspectives range from an engaged young woman in her mid-twenties to a seasoned couple who have been married for fifty-five years, as well as experienced, professional colleagues. These people include: Merilee Tanner Thompson, Sam and Christie Preisler, Gary Steggell, Bret and Amy Harmon, Mick Epperson, Eddie and Wilma Sadleir, Bill Tanner, and Sue Jones.

CONTENTS

PREFACE

O_N JANUARY 1970, I decided to pursue a vocation that would help me strengthen families. Although I've done many things consistent with this career objective, I've come to believe that there simply is not a more important way to realize my personal, professional mission in life than to help the basic unit of families—the husband and wife team—learn how to strengthen their core relationship with one another.

In reflecting upon the twenty-five years of doing both "preventive" and "rehabilitative" work with couples, I found that I have typically operated according to the same basic premise: What people need is to learn how to make their marriage work. Whether they are enthusiastic about enriching their marriage or desperately striving to salvage it, all couples must learn the same timeless principles and apply the same proven practices for successful relationships. In our information age, I'm convinced that the vast majority of men and women today—now more than ever—need and want to know what works, so they can make it work for themselves.

The concluding statement in the doctoral dissertation I wrote to earn a Ph.D. in Family Relations was this sentence: "Structuring activities which encourage people to interact frequently and regularly with their loved ones is an important first step; *teaching them how to love each other is the journey which must follow.*" [Emphasis added.] Twenty-two years after coming to that conclusion, after extensive opportunities to develop and refine my thinking on this subject as it relates to couples, I have finally written with my wife, Susan, *Enjoy the Journey Along Your Marriage Highway.* Our hope is that this self-help book will help fill an important need by teaching husbands and wives how to love each other in ways that really count. The *Six Practices* encompass all the essentials of what it takes to develop and maintain a satisfying and lasting relationship. We are confident that this book—along with the accompanying *KISS Marriage Maker*™—are resources that can assist you and your partner to experience joy.

If reading this book helps you avoid some of the pitfalls along the sometimes rocky road of marriage, Susan and I will feel like our efforts to write the book will have been worthwhile. For readers who discover ways to actually make their marriage better than it was before, we will be thrilled. And for those couples who are willing to invest in their relationship enough to learn and regularly apply all *Six Practices,* we will enjoy the deep and abiding satisfaction that comes from knowing we've made a real difference. That's because these husbands and wives—and hopefully this includes the two of you—will reap the rewards of a truly *thriving* marriage!

We invite you to use this "handbook" while you travel *Along Your Marriage Highway* as one way to *Nurture Joy Forever.* Our sincere desire is that you will both *Enjoy the Journey!*

Tres and Susan Tanner
San Diego, California
July 1997

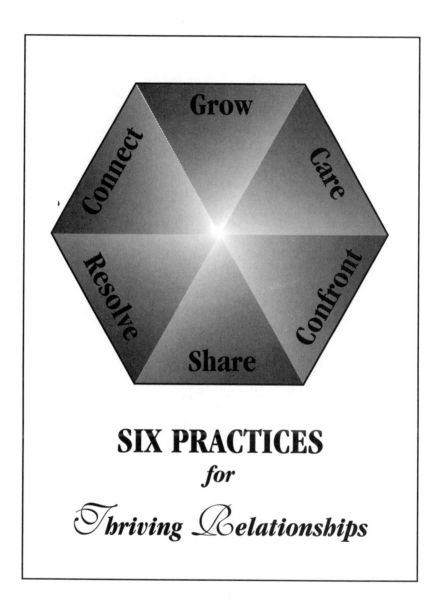

SIX PRACTICES
for
Thriving Relationships

"Grief can take care of itself; but to get the
full measure of joy, you must have
somebody to share it with."

— *Mark Twain* —

1

BEGINNINGS

Learn to Enjoy the Journey
on Your Marriage Highway

$\mathcal{M}$ARRIAGE is like a journey with lots of milestones along the way. Many couples don't enjoy their trip because they are continually looking toward some destination point and thinking that once they reach it, they'll be happy. "We'll be happy when we: get married . . . graduate . . . buy our dream home . . . have a baby . . . have more money . . . take that special vacation together . . . retire . . ." The problem is, these destination points come and go, and sometimes we recognize a dramatic change in our lives, but other times we do not.

Mostly, we transition from one challenge or issue to another. If we are always focused on a milestone further up the road, or on what we think is a final destination, we lose opportunities for happiness along the way. Another reason we are sometimes unhappy is that when we run into tough times in our relationship, we allow the difficulties to negatively affect our feelings toward each other. We then presume that marital happiness is somehow equated with the absence of problems. According to this view, any rough spots naturally would detract from our happiness together. In the short run, this mistaken belief can only diminish our capacity to enjoy our relationship, and over a lifetime it can bring much sorrow and resentment.

Of course husbands and wives will face problems! Difficulties are part and parcel of the human condition and certainly come with the territory in married life, as well.

You can expect to continually face difficulties, so it's crucial to reinforce a healthy attitude about the potholes and bumpy stretches of road along your marriage highway.

We simply should not allow any obstacle to undermine our happiness. If we view stumbling blocks as stepping stones, and problems as challenges to master and grow from, we can expect to enjoy our journey no matter what trials we may go through. For example, working together to overcome a major financial loss can contribute to our joy just as much as going on a special vacation together. Marital happiness need not be an elusive butterfly. We can experience joy together as we learn to:

1. Apply correct principles in our relationship, and

2. Recognize and relish our moments of joy.

1. Apply Correct Principles

Webster's Dictionary defines joy as "intense happiness or great delight." However, real joy can never be felt merely as the result of happy events in our lives. Although our joy can include pleasure, satisfaction, and happiness, real joy is on a higher plane. Joy is experienced in the depth of our souls as we live consistent with our sound beliefs and core values. When both partners live correct principles, our life together can be a joyful experience to treasure. In this sense, joy is really a result of the serenity and inner peace that come from knowing that the choices we're making and the life we're living benefit ourselves and everyone around us.

Fairy tale endings distort a wonderful truth. Adults—who were thrilled as children with tales of the prince and princess getting married and living "happily ever after"—

become disenchanted as they discover marriage just isn't that simple. Life is relentless in throwing "stuff" at us. It doesn't always matter whether this stuff is bad, neutral, or even good; it's just that the sheer quantity of what we have to deal with can so consume our emotional, mental, and physical energies that sometimes we have nothing left. This makes it almost impossible for any man and woman to live "happily ever after" in the storybook sense. But when a husband and wife understand and internalize the essence of real joy, they can live "joyfully ever after" as they savor their moments of joy and implement correct principles in their marriage.

Each chapter in this book will focus on different marriage joys and proven principles for effective relationships. As you read each chapter, consider ways you can apply the specific practice and the corresponding correct principles to create real joy in your relationship. This is how you can learn to *Enjoy the Journey Along Your Marriage Highway!*

2. Experience Moments of Joy

*S*USAN:

    Tres is one of the most upbeat people I've ever known, and he finds joy every day of his life. Recently he said to me, "I wish you could feel more joy in your life." In reflecting on his comment, the thought struck me: I had become so caught up in the activities of living and working, I rarely thought about—much less appreciated—all the moments of joy I was experiencing every day. It was not that I was unhappy, but I wasn't feeling the joy along the way.

    I decided I needed to define, in my own mind, what moments contribute to my happiness. Too many of us think of joyful moments primarily as those major "kick up your heels" experiences. Moments of joy, however, are not just major life events, but can come from any pleasant experience, however small. Some joyful moments for me include: walking in the warm sunshine, planting flowers, watching our grown children talk and laugh the way they did as little children, experiencing the smell of baking bread, lying next to Tres and feeling the warmth of his body, receiving a simple hug and kiss from him after a long day, or laughing at a dumb joke.

Now, I make it a point to recognize my moments of joy, relish the feelings they create within me, and share them with my sweetheart.

Our moments of joy and the feelings associated with them can be difficult to recognize because they are often intangible. To make these moments of joy more real for you, identify what activities and experiences make you feel good, so you can more readily recognize them as they happen. It's not possible to identify every moment of joy before it happens, but thinking about the types of things that make you happy can help you recognize the spontaneous ones as they occur. Take the time to truly appreciate and be thankful for them. The experiences become more meaningful as you share your feelings about them with your sweetheart. By describing or discussing them, you make the feelings and the experiences more tangible, and thus more real.

*S*USAN:

One day as Tres and I were driving along a road, a major storm began moving into the valley. I was listening to the radio as I noticed how incredible the clouds were with the various shades of gray and black contrasted against the newly budding green of the trees in spring. It almost took my breath away, and I felt such awe at the beauty of the world around me. It was truly a moment of joy I would never have put on my list of things I enjoy, but I recognized the feelings within me and shared them with Tres. He, too, recognized the beauty, and we discussed the shades of colors that contributed to the mystic atmosphere of this spring storm. By talking about, describing, and sharing how it made us feel, the experience became very tangible and more special to both of us, as it became a recognized moment of joy.

If you want to make the most of life's joyful moments:
- Identify any experiences or things that make you feel good inside (bring you joy).
- Savor these whenever they occur.
- Express your feelings about them to your companion.

Having fun with our partner—fun usually spawned by external events—makes our relationships much more enjoyable. But real joy—which is felt deep within us—is the key to relationships that are truly satisfying.

Who Is This Book For?

For any of you who are content to merely survive marriage or "get by" in your relationship—and there are millions in this category—you might as well stop right here. This book will do you no good.

For those of you who believe, or at least hope, it is possible to experience deep satisfaction and find joy along your way—read on. This book is for you.

Throughout our life journey, we all travel along one path or another. Most adults would like to share their trip with a special traveling companion. These individuals get on the Highway of Marriage and, sooner or later, recognize that this road is not easy to travel. The Marriage Highway is just that—a *high* way, demanding a high level of commitment from its travelers in return for the great rewards it potentially offers.

And just what are they like—those who pursue this path in life's journey? As a matter of fact, there are all kinds of travelers on the Marriage Highway. Some of you have "only just begun" your trip down the road as a couple. You hope for a wonderful trek. Many of you may have been hiking, jogging, or inching your way down the highways and byways of your marriage for years—often stumbling, occasionally sprinting, and at times just barely crawling. A number of you have stuck it out through thick and thin, for better or worse, for decades. Since you're very committed to each other as traveling companions, you'd like to find a better way to travel.

Still others have fallen—or jumped—off the course of marriage before; maybe several times. You know only too well that marriage can be a long and dreary road of unhappiness and pain. You have lots of scars from serious accidents on the road. Some of you are terrified at the thought of ever traveling again; all have doubts aplenty. Nevertheless, you're hoping that maybe, just maybe, you can learn to "get it right" this time.

Then there are those travelers who have never set foot on the marriage path. You have always been single and may or may not be currently involved in a significant relationship. You've watched too many friends or family members crash on the road. Many of you are extremely doubtful about whether it's possible for any couple to survive the journey, much less experience anything close to marital bliss. You think it's better to stay off the road altogether. Perhaps you steer clear of any involvement with those of the opposite gender. On the other hand, you may have chosen a parallel path; you're traveling the frontage road of a quasi-marriage relationship with someone to whom you're not yet married. Your perspective: "Oh yeah? . . . Show me."

For all who travel the Marriage Highway—or are considering taking up the journey—our message is pretty much the same: There is no royal road of marriage. Anyone who has ever set foot on this path (or watched others from the sidelines) knows that the course is strewn with boulders, filled with plenty of unexpected, bone-jarring potholes, and characterized by messy, muddy stretches of road and steep drop-offs on practically every curve. Many feel there is very little happiness—much less joy—along this road.

On the other hand, some travelers foolishly believe they can simply frolic along this road as if it were a forest footpath. They are mistaken. Traveling along the Highway of Marriage can and ought to be a joyful journey, with plenty of opportunities for playful romping and spontaneous sauntering along the way. But the *high* way of marriage is a serious course that calls for partners who are highly committed traveling companions. Accidental tourists who think they can simply stroll or aimlessly wander along the way will never fare well on this purposeful path.

The good news? The trip is worth it.

Whether you are young, enthusiastic hikers, seasoned travelers, or battle-scarred road warriors, this is a handbook for marriage travelers to help you enjoy the journey. You'll learn about avoiding hazards along the way. Our emphasis is to help you learn the "Rules of the Road" that we refer to as *practices*. Following these rules will bring you the happiness you deserve. They will assist you in identifying, recognizing, and savoring joy, so you can enjoy the journey.

Why Do You Need This Book?

It's no secret that families today are being bombarded from every side. Under the pressures of the siege, many are ripped apart, or left with only a few torn and tattered edges. At the center of this attack is the very foundation of every family—the couple.

Here's an unfortunate fact of life for husbands and wives today: To assume that your marriage can endure anything, or that your love will keep you together "no matter what," is both naive and short-sighted. Wise couples need to be constantly on guard against the many forces that undermine the husband-wife relationship. Sometimes the attack is a full frontal assault, like your mate being tempted by a flirtatious co-worker. Other times husbands and wives are their own worst enemies, as when one spouse repeatedly attacks the self-esteem of the other. Even the best relationships can be destroyed, and, unfortunately, every marriage is vulnerable. Fortunately, every marriage partner can learn the principles to fortify and deepen his or her core relationship in life. This book was written to help you do just that.

Successful marriage is not something we can simply decide we want, work to achieve, and then assume will remain like some shiny award in our trophy case. Marriage is a relationship. As such, it is dynamic and continually evolving. With effort and patience, any husband and wife can work together to develop a very satisfying marriage. For it to endure this way means that both partners must continue to nurture it forever.

Every couple committed to keeping a happy marriage from becoming a divorce statistic needs to be serious and effective in combining the efforts of both husband and wife to create and maintain a strong, enduring relationship. Concerning the need for the active participation of *both* spouses, remember these two sobering realities: (a) It only takes *one* disaffected spouse to end a marriage; (b) with persistent effort, *one* committed partner can help a couple sustain their relationship endlessly on a "surviving" level, but achieving and maintaining a "thriving" marriage always requires the active involvement of *both* mates.

Although it has become an all-too-common occurrence, divorce is not inevitable. Marriages break up for many reasons, but mostly because couples allow it to happen. It's quite rare that the downfall of a relationship is the result of a single blow, no matter how hard. More often, marital dissolution is just that—a marriage that has dissolved and deteriorated over time.

This happens when partners fail to recognize their personal responsibility to relate to each other in ways that are pleasing to both, and to bring out the best in one another. In organizational development circles, another new buzz-word has become fashionable: "responsibility leadership." This term suggests that individuals need to assume more personal responsibility for what happens and quit using the lame crutches of blame or excuses. The same is true for marriage.

Married or not, many couples never establish any expectations about the quality of their relationship. Instead, they merely "hope it will work out." How sad! As with anything we value in life, we need to determine whether we want it badly enough to invest our time and energy into making it work. As long as you're going to spend your life together, why not choose to have a great marriage?

A quality marriage requires both high expectations and a corresponding level of effort to implement correct principles. Achieving a successful marriage is no different than achieving success in any other area of life. Marriage, too, is subject to the "Law of the Harvest"; we can only expect to reap what we sow. In other words, we cannot receive the rich rewards of a truly thriving marriage unless we earn them. We must learn what to do, and then do what it takes. This does not have to be perceived as a chore, and you'll see as you read this book how to enjoy the journey.

Life is a classroom, and we are continually learning and growing. Unfortunately, in the classroom of life, we tend to be given our test first, and later must learn the lessons given on the test. This can be a very painful process. How much better it would be if we could learn some of the essential lessons about marriage before we were given our tests on the subject! This book can help you through your tests by teaching some of these vital lessons.

*S*USAN:

Last summer, one of our young friends, a bright and capable young adult, got married to her sweetheart. They had gotten along fine during the eighteen months of their relationship, had never really had any serious conflicts or fights, and had thought life would be wonderful and that they would live "happily ever after" once they got married. But, six months after the wedding, she called in tears, wondering what had happened and why her husband had changed so much since their wedding. She couldn't understand what seemed to be the dramatic differences in the ways they related to each other. She thought that because there was conflict and disagreement, there must be something wrong with their relationship.

I certainly didn't have all the answers, but I asked her, "Do you love him?" The young woman answered, "Yes." I asked her how much she had read or knew about some of their challenge areas such as confronting problems, dealing with the differences between them, or resolving conflicts. She admitted she did not know very much, and that she hadn't read anything that might help her understand how to do that.

Over the years, the young woman had won numerous trophies and awards for showing her horse. She had never been able to afford to pay a trainer and was rightfully very proud of the fact that she had studied hard, reading every magazine she could get her hands on about training and showing horses. I asked her, "Would you have won the trophies if you hadn't made the effort to learn all you could about horses?" "Of course not," she replied. After a pause, I said, "You know, marriage isn't much different. To succeed in marriage, we all need to learn how to develop the kind of relationship we want. It doesn't necessarily come naturally."

That made sense to her, and she agreed she needed to read and learn everything she could to better understand what was happening between them, as well as what they could do to make their marriage better. (I made it very clear I was not comparing her husband to her horse nor recommending that she read up on "how to train a husband!")

Ironically, though, learning how to make a marriage work can be somewhat confusing.

Go into any bookstore and you'll find dozens of books and tapes related to marriage or some aspect of marriage. Besides those which focus on marriage itself, they cover topics such as needs, roles, effective listening, gender differences, improving your sex life, love—the list goes on. This material provides couples with countless ways to understand a wide variety of perspectives about the most important of human relationships—that between a man and a woman.

However, like most people today, you probably don't have time to sort through all the information available. Although it might be interesting to explore the numerous

Why should we bother reading something if we can't—or won't— apply it to actually improving and benefiting our marriage?

dimensions of marriage, it's just not realistic, which is precisely why we wrote this book. Our intention was to include in a single volume a summary of the essential components for a successful marriage. It's designed for busy people like you. It will help you focus on what really works—a handbook you can refer back to as often as necessary as a reminder and reinforcer of the practices you can internalize.

RES:

As one whose education and career has centered around families and children, I have benefitted greatly from the insightful perspectives, memorable stories, and practical suggestions made by scores of authors in hundreds of books and tapes. (As a counselor, I often assigned clients to read a book that covered a certain topic far better and more efficiently than I ever could in a counseling session.) Susan and I certainly encourage you to take advantage of the great blessing of living in "The Information Age" by using whatever books, tapes, or programs will help you learn more about specific facets of your relationship—especially those that offer practical suggestions which will actually improve your marriage.

To succeed in marriage in today's fast-paced, complex world, as a couple you must:

> **1. Learn the proven, tested ideas that really make a difference.**
>
> **2. Apply these practices on an ongoing basis in your relationship with one another.**

Throughout the book, you'll understand the basic principles and concepts (the *whats* and *whys*) as well as learn a variety of practical methods (the *hows*) that you and your mate can apply in your everyday life. We encourage couples to move from a "So what?" orientation to a "Now what?" response to these ideas. After all, since most of us have so little time and so much information available, it's reasonable to ask ourselves: "Why should we bother reading something if we can't—or won't—apply it to improve and benefit our marriage?" Whether you find this book to be a source of new insights, different perspectives on familiar themes, or reminders to do more of what you already know works, *Enjoy the Journey Along Your Marriage Highway* can help you and your partner.

There's a current trend in the business world to focus on the "best practices" used by successful organizations in each industry. The idea is to identify what has worked most successfully for others, and then emulate it. (In today's world, who has time to "reinvent the wheel"?) This book is our summary of the best practices that all successful couples must apply in their marriage relationships.

What's in the Book?

So, just what are these "practices," and where did they come from? For our purposes, we will define practices as the core principles which, when applied by both partners, lead to satisfying, enduring marriage relationships.

Identifying *The Six Practices for Thriving Relationships* is our way of summarizing a fairly comprehensive distillation of the vitally important things that husbands and wives must do in order to cultivate and maintain a vibrant, lasting relationship. It is based primarily upon Tres's work with thousands of people over a period of twenty-five years as a marriage counselor, conducting marriage enrichment retreats, teaching college courses in marriage and family relationships, observations and conversations with husbands and wives, and his own experiences in marriage. In reflecting upon these experiences, our objective was to organize these ideas into a simple, unified framework that would be relatively easy for couples to learn and remember.

It turns out that virtually all the essential factors partners must understand and apply in their relationships can be grouped into six broad categories. After developing the initial framework, Tres tested, developed, and refined them in four different contexts: (1) with undergraduate students in several college courses in marriage and family relations; (2) with masters and doctoral students in a graduate practicum in marriage and family therapy; (3) with clients engaged in personal and group marriage counseling, and (4) with couples in seminars.

The *Six Practices* are very basic in the sense that they are not tied to gender. That is, each *practice* is equally important for both the man and the woman to apply in order to achieve an excellent relationship with one another. This is only logical, since marriage is a relationship involving both a husband and a wife—neither one acting alone.

The hexagon design is used with *The Six Practices for Thriving Relationships* framework as a visual reminder that each practice is like one of the facets of a jewel. Couples can always work to enhance or "polish" each of these facets in their relationship. When a couple consistently applies all six practices, they will enjoy their jewel of a thriving marriage, which will actually be a unique and precious gem, just as the two of them are unique and precious individuals. *(See figure on page 14 and those found at the beginning of each chapter.)*

Originally, I referred to them as the "Six Practices for a Thriving Marriage." We changed the name to *The Six Practices for Thriving Relationships* for two reasons. One was in realizing that many couples who can benefit from this book are not married, such as engaged couples or those who may be living together but unmarried. Unmarried couples will find that the same practices still apply to their relationship. (Some such partners might just discover, as they begin to experience the positive results from applying the *Six Practices*, that they want to enjoy the benefits of a fully committed marriage.) The other reason is that many of the ideas described in this book—while oriented primarily to couples in their core relationship—can also be applied beneficially in other relationships in their lives.

The Six Practices for Thriving Relationships Are:

1. Share: Spend time in new and renewed shared experiences with your chosen companion.

2. Care: Nurture a best-friends relationship with your husband or wife.

3. Connect: Enhance the emotional and physical intimacy with your "soulmate."

4. Confront: Communicate concerns about "tough stuff" with your spouse.

5. Resolve: Deal with differences and resolve conflicts with your helpmate.

6. Grow: Refine the shared vision and spousal synergy with your life partner.

A chapter has been devoted to each of these practices. Each chapter will explain the *whats* and *whys*, as well as describe the practical *hows* that you and your mate can apply in your everyday life. We recognize that you might not automatically accept these practices just because you have read them in this book. Instead, we challenge you to put them to the test: Implement these principles in your lives, and you will experience the difference they can make in your relationship. Plant the seed, nurture it, and watch it grow!

Think of the practices as the basic building blocks for your marriage. With each marital practice you apply, you are building a stronger relationship, one that will help you withstand whatever life throws at you. The interrelationship between the practices is emphasized by the sequence of chapters. The *Six Practices* are described in the book in the same approximate order that most relationships develop when two people meet. After couples have some *shared* experiences, they begin to *care* for each other. They then start *connecting* with deeper levels of emotional and physical intimacy. Ultimately, however, every couple must learn to *confront* their difficult issues and *resolve* their conflicts. Finally, partners need to feel they are continually *growing*—both as individuals and as a couple.

In your efforts to rebuild or strengthen a faltering relationship, you can greatly improve your chances by following this natural sequence. When you begin the healing process, you should focus first on the simpler, more positive steps of spending time together, caring for and connecting with one another. This will help you restore better feelings for each other so you're more likely to succeed in addressing the tougher issues in your relationship, such as confronting and resolving problems. (The importance of this sequence, as well as some very useful methods to help couples accomplish this, are described in Richard Stuart's book for marriage counselors, *Helping Couples Change.*)

Unfortunately, the vast majority of husbands and wives never even come close to applying the *Grow* practice— what we sometimes refer to as the "icing" on the cake of marriage. As you learn about growing together, you'll realize it's not necessarily difficult, but requires a consciousness and awareness of what growing together is all about. Nevertheless, partners committed to thriving relationships make sure they implement all six practices throughout their marriage.

All six practices build upon and are interrelated to one another. Thus, you'll notice that different chapters may deal with similar issues in more depth or from a different angle. For example, there is a natural link between nurturing a "best-friends" relationship described in the *Care* chapter and enhancing emotional intimacy described in the *Connect* chapter. Cultivating a close friendship helps our willingness to be emotionally vulnerable, so we can open up and share our deeper inner feelings—the essence of emotional intimacy. Likewise, as couples learn to skillfully confront the difficult issues in their relationship, they are much better prepared to resolve their challenges effectively.

As you read this book, you'll discover that many of the ideas presented are not totally new. This is to be expected. In virtually every aspect of human relationships, those principles and practices which are effective have been used by people in many cultures for centuries. Because this book is a distillation of proven practices, it's only natural that some of what you read will seem familiar. If you find that the ideas in *Enjoy the Journey Along Your Marriage Highway* strike a familiar chord, we'll be pleased. If you say to yourselves, "Gee, we're applying that idea already," we'll be grateful this book can confirm that you are doing many things "right."

> ***In this book, "communication" is considered an underlying <u>process</u> rather than a <u>practice</u>.***

Most marriage books include communication as one of the key ingredients for success. In our book, however, we have not identified this as one of the *Six Practices*. This isn't because communication is unimportant, but rather we see it as a basic, underlying process used to implement each practice. In order to successfully engage in shared activities, care for each other, connect physically and emotionally, confront challenges, resolve conflicts, and grow together, couples need to be able to effectively use a variety of verbal and nonverbal communication skills. So, in reading this book, remember that communication is viewed as an essential process rather than a practice.

We have also not included "love" as one of the *Six Practices.* Although love is essential in all good marriages, it's a concept which, unfortunately, has lost some of its usefulness simply because it has come to mean so many different things to so many people and is sometimes used superficially. Nevertheless, as couples *share, care, connect, confront, resolve,* and *grow* in their relationship, in reality they are demonstrating their love for one another in ways that really make a difference.

How Do You Use This Book?

Some relationship books are designed for readers to sit down on a beach and read straight through, without needing to stop and contemplate, discuss, or apply. Certain books are full of insightful observations and compelling anecdotes readers can relate to, while others have an exclusively "how-to" orientation.

> ### This book is not intended to be simply _informational_, but, rather, _transformational._

We had a different purpose, however, in writing this book. Our objective was twofold: (1) teach key concepts, and (2) provide practical ways to implement those concepts. The essential concepts are organized into six basic categories that you can readily review and internalize. This book certainly can be read straight through. And although a reader can gain much information by reading its contents on a plane, in a waiting room, or on the beach, it was never intended to be just a "beach read." *Enjoy the Journey Along*

Your Marriage Highway is not designed to be merely interesting reading on relationships in general, but beneficial to your own special relationship. It is not intended to be simply *informa*tional, but rather *transforma*tional.

This book has also been written to accommodate two reading styles. Those who want a thorough understanding of the content can read the entire book. For those who feel they don't have the time—or simply prefer to scan the highlights—we've made this easy by including in each chapter:

- Highlights of key concepts throughout each chapter, and at the end of each chapter.
- A summary of main ideas.
- A series of 20 questions to ponder and discuss.
- A list of suggested ideas to consider.

Those who prefer more structure or a step-by-step, "self-help" approach should review the various alternatives outlined in *Appendix B*. The key is to adapt the book to your own unique needs.

20 Questions

Remember the game "Twenty Questions"? At the end of each chapter is a series of *20 Questions to Ponder and Discuss*. The purpose of these questions is to help readers evaluate how well they're applying a specific practice. If both partners answer the questions individually and then discuss these questions with one another, it will help them focus their efforts on that particular practice. These questions are not intended as a way to judge yourself or your mate for any ways you might be falling short. Rather, they are included as an additional way to help you determine how you can most effectively use your time and energy to improve your relationship.

We are all exposed to hundreds of good ideas that we never apply and which, therefore, don't really benefit us much. In the *20 Questions* section of each chapter, question #20 encourages you to consider other worthwhile ideas you've learned about the practice. This could be from a variety of sources: other books or tapes, movies, music, plays, observations of other couples—there is no limit to the ways we can learn useful information. What this book can do is help you organize your thinking and plan actions to make your relationship even better.

Suppose you saw a movie that really made an impression on you about healing relationships. In this film, imagine that the couple is able to build a deeper friendship once one of the partners is willing to let go of a long-held resentment and sincerely forgive his or her mate. You might share your feelings about this with your companion as you review Question #20 in the *Care* chapter, and possibly even discuss how you can work on learning to let go of resentments and become more forgiving. In this way, these tools will have helped you transform daily learning opportunities into meaningful results in your own relationship.

An Ongoing Process

Clarifying what it is you want and taking the steps to make it happen is an ongoing process—not a single event that will happen immediately. This book does not offer a "quick fix" approach. Instead, it teaches concepts and provides tools to help you continually refine and nurture your marriage. Those who wish to get the greatest return on their investment may find themselves referring to the book frequently during the course of their marriage, rather than simply reading it once. Whenever we learn vital principles about any topic we consider important, it sometimes helps to periodically remind ourselves of the essentials about such principles.

You may be part of a relationship wherein you have learned many of these practices, but your partner has not. Even if only one of you is willing to learn and apply the principles, the principles still can have a real impact on your relationship. However, to gain the maximum benefit from this book, we recommend that you do the following:

1. Read the book *together.*
2. Discuss the ideas *together.*
3. Set application goals *together.*
4. Evaluate your progress *together.*

Our commitment is to ensure that you're not only aware of the essential knowledge, but also have a practical way to apply it frequently. This way, it can make a real difference in your marriage. In order to make the "Now What" component easier, we've provided a simple tool to help you establish, and follow through with, weekly goals related to *The Six Practices.* It's called the *KISS Marriage Maker*™. In some ways, this resource is even more important than the book, because it will help you take proven, practical ideas off the pages, through your mind, and into your life. For this reason, even "scanners" may want to do a quick read of *Appendix A,* which explains this simple tool.

Use the __KISS Marriage Maker__™ to take these ideas off the pages, through your mind, and into your life.

℘RES:

I've gained some interesting insights by observing individuals who work out in health clubs, and the personal trainers who help them. See if you recognize the significant parallels with marriage relationships.

Of the dozens of people in a gym working out at any given time, each individual has his or her own personal fitness goals. Some are trying to lose weight, some want to increase their cardiovascular endurance or their strength, and others want to tone and firm up or simply maintain their fitness level. Each individual is at a different place in his or her own progress relative to personal fitness goals. Some have just started and others have been at it for years. These people approach their programs differently with respect to the intensity (how hard they work at it) and regularity (how frequently they exercise). Patrons can use different machines and workout exercises depending on their specific fitness objectives. Each has his or her own reason for being there, personal objectives, and degree of involvement in this aspect of self-improvement.

The reality is, even the most dedicated "fitness buffs" have interruptions and setbacks along the way toward their goals; that's life. An individual who may have planned a daily workout of one hour may have to modify his involvement during a busy week and might be lucky if he can squeeze in a couple of 20-minute sessions on the treadmill.

At these fitness clubs, the overall climate is generally one of mutual respect and supportiveness among the patrons. All recognize that every person at the club is at some level of fitness—some are exceptionally fit, and others, like me, need a lot of work to get into shape. Rather than judging others, comparing or competing, most are likely to offer encouragement to any person who is making an effort to improve. Those who have just begun the process are especially supported and encouraged.

Consider this analogy as you work on improving your own "marriage fitness." Remember these two points: (a) Your relationship will benefit greatly as you work on it regularly—this book will show you how to do this; (b) be patient with yourself and your mate. All couples striving to make their marriage better deserve all the support they can get.

Every marriage has its relative weaknesses and strengths. For example, some couples might do a great job of sharing mutual interests and experiences, but don't feel close to one another. Others may have a great sex life, but don't treat each other as real friends. Still other partners treat one another kindly, but have never learned to confront their challenges constructively or to resolve their differences effectively. The emphasis you give each practice is, of course, completely up to you as a couple. To enjoy the journey, determine how you want your relationship to be, and then proceed down the highway together.

In today's troubled times, we applaud all who have the courage to be on the Highway of Marriage at all! For those who are afraid, skeptical, or hesitant to get on the trail, we encourage you to take the first step, and then learn how to make progress—one step at a time. For all current and potential travelers who want to achieve success and happiness as you travel along your own unique path, we invite you to use *Enjoy the Journey Along Your Marriage Highway* and the *KISS Marriage Maker*™ tool. Our sincere hope is that, in some small way, these might help you enjoy your journey together!

We wish both of you much joy in the lifelong process of developing the kind of satisfying, enduring and thriving marriage your relationship was meant to be!

"To be with those I like is enough."

— *Walt Whitman* —

2

SHARE

*Spend Time in New and
Renewed Shared Experiences
with Your Chosen Companion*

---

*C*A PRIMARY reason people marry is to share their lives with the special companion they've chosen. This includes couples who've been married for decades, as well as the current generation of young people. These "twenty-something" couples have expressed their views quite clearly on this subject in interviews and polls: In today's increasingly uncertain world, they would like to share their lives with a companion. They prefer to face many of their challenges together early on, rather than go through them alone, or wait until their individual careers, personalities and social lives are firmly entrenched. It's almost as though, instead of sarcastically urging others to "Get a life," they prefer to enthusiastically encourage individuals to "Share your life!" Unfortunately, too many of us—of any age—seem to forget that our spouse is actually the individual whom we once chose to share our life with.

When a man and woman first meet, they usually begin to share experiences based on common interests or activities they enjoy. Thus, shared experiences are natural in the early phase of their relationship as they go out and explore life together. This is one way people determine whether they enjoy similar things and are compatible with each other.

Remember when the two of you first met? Did you want to spend every minute together? When we first met, we couldn't stand to be apart; even short separations seemed like an eternity. We went everywhere together, even grocery shopping. Life just seemed so much better when we were together doing everyday things. Joy came easily and naturally. Of course, we're not naive enough to expect that this intensity persists throughout the course of a relationship. Nevertheless, most of us know of couples who, after twenty, thirty, or forty years of marriage, still prefer to be together as much as possible. As best friends, we continue to enjoy being around each other, so we look for opportunities to spend as much of our time together as possible. Whether it's running errands, cleaning the house, fixing a meal, picking out clothes or furniture, planting flowers, or doing some kind of decorating or home improvement project doesn't really matter. What does matter is that we find ways through small, ordinary experiences to share our lives together.

Some couples feel that as harried as life gets, the only way they can share time is to plan for an occasional getaway together. Getaways are great; all couples can benefit by going off for a few days to some special place for recreation and fun. But shared experiences need not be recreational or fun to serve an important function in marriage. Life itself requires us to engage in a variety of daily tasks. Shopping, preparing food, doing the laundry, caring for the home—the list is endless. Husbands and wives are sometimes surprised at how much more of their limited time can be spent together when they include among their shared experiences those necessary activities called "work." When marriage partners fold clothes, prepare meals, wash dishes, rake leaves, weed, or paint a room together once in a while, they're much more likely to feel like companions in life.

Some observers have noted that our modern, time-saving conveniences, like microwaves and dishwashers, can, ironically, deprive us of time that couples used to spend together. Susan can recall spending hours washing dishes with her mother and brother. They talked and laughed as they tried to make the mundane, boring job more fun. This same concept can be applied as couples consciously make the time spent in tedious jobs more fun and rewarding. You might be surprised how something simple like washing and drying your dishes by hand together could lead to more conversations, more laughter, and more joy!

In essence, *Share* is all about spending time together. After all, it's only when you are with your mate that you can actually share your life with this person! As you read the other chapters in this book, you will understand how the *Share* practice relates to each of the other practices. It's only when partners are together that they can nurture a best-friends relationship (*Care*), enhance their intimacy (*Connect*), communicate their concerns about tough stuff (*Confront*), deal with their differences and resolve their conflicts (*Resolve*), and refine their shared vision and synergy together (*Grow*). Remember, there needs to be a balance of our time spent together, time spent with others, and time spent alone.

Even though we need to ensure adequate time together, we can sometimes make the mistake of believing that our marriage partners can fulfill all of our needs, which they cannot. No one person can. This is unrealistic and unfair to our mates and ourselves. We all enjoy doing some things with people other than our spouses. Besides, for rich, full, balanced lives, we all need to find ways to enjoy the unique benefits of interacting with a variety of individuals. Spending time with other people helps us develop new ideas and perspectives and can help us achieve an even better relationship.

We also need to recognize the value of time alone, enjoying activities that each one finds personally satisfying, such as going to the gym, reading books, working on old cars, or gardening. This helps each partner feel they are retaining and building upon their unique identity as individuals, in addition to the time they spend in their roles as husband or wife.

Sometimes, however, these personal activities consume so much of our free time that time spent together is seriously compromised. Thus, some marriages begin to drift apart. Because we lead such busy lives, it is critical to maintain a reasonable balance between the time spent in personal and couple activities if we want to feel like our spouse is actually our life companion. One solution is to convert a personal activity into one enjoyed by both parties.

ᏚRES:

One experience that Susan and I enjoy together is going for evening walks. This began when she invited me to join her in a daily routine she'd developed over the years to unwind from the stresses of the day, get some good exercise, and enjoy meditating and praying while she walked under the stars.

As the two of us began walking together, our walks became frequent opportunities for us to talk with one another, share our dreams, and sort through problems together. So, what had previously been an individual experience for Susan became a very worthwhile, renewed, shared experience for both of us, which we sometimes refer to as our "walk-talks." She still enjoys walking alone sometimes, so I always ask her if this is a night she prefers to walk alone, or if I should join her. She always lets me know, and I'm not offended when she says, "I need to walk alone tonight."

Because of our busy lives, many of which are spent working or doing things with others, it's easy to feel resentful when it seems our mates spend little of their time with us. But it usually doesn't do much good to criticize your spouse for "never spending time with me." Instead, focus your energies on two things: First, plan activities that the two of you might especially enjoy. Second, ensure that when you are together, you make it a point to interact in ways that make you glad to be in each other's company. Some couples return from a vacation together even more tense than before, because even though they were with each other 100 percent of the time, it was filled with mostly unpleasant interaction. Whether it's a vacation or doing chores together, what counts is the quality of the time you spend together. Nevertheless, structuring time to share as companions is a first step.

This leads to an interesting point: Just because the two of you are together doesn't mean that you are sharing your life. Consider this: Some husbands and wives feel that when they both come home after a tiring day, spending an evening together in front of the TV or watching videos is sharing. Wrong. Here's why: Those who study preschoolers have long observed that one kind of play children engage in is called "parallel play," like when two children sit in a sandbox, each one playing with their own toys by themselves. Although they are doing the same thing, they are not doing it together. While this kind of play certainly has its value, there is no social benefit because the children never interact with one another.

In similar fashion, we all benefit from the ways television can entertain us, educate us, or help us unwind. But remember, even when both of us are watching TV together, unless we make it a point to talk about what we're watching, this activity will do nothing for our relationship, and certainly is not sharing as we've described it. That's how television—whether it's a small box or a huge screen—has the potential to indirectly and gradually, without anyone ever really being aware of it, become a destructive force in millions of marriages. It's also why wise couples make it a point to not allow the habit of watching television to rob them of the limited, precious time they could otherwise share with one another. Many couples find they have more time than they imagined to actively share their lives together when they reclaim some of the hours they previously spent in "parallel passivity" watching TV.

Now that we've reviewed *why* we need to share life together, let's discuss two specific types of shared experiences. All couples need to: (a) share new activities together that are interesting and stimulating; and (b) renew their feelings

by sharing activities they've enjoyed during the entire
course of their relationship.

New Experiences

Sharing experiences allows us to create new memories
together, keep the relationship growing, and keep it from
getting stale. Remember the hit single "Escape" (the "Piña
Colada" song by Rupert Holmes)? The husband complains
about how he and his lady have gotten into the same old,
dull routine. He loves her, but is bored with their relationship; it has become routine and stale. So he responds to a
personal ad in the newspaper: "If
you like piña coladas, getting
caught in the rain; If you're not into
yoga; if you're into champagne . . ."
and continues to describe activities that he wants to share with
someone. When he finally meets
the woman to whom he has
responded, he is both surprised
and delighted to see that she is
his "own lovely lady." He then
says he didn't know "that you liked piña coladas, getting
caught in the rain . . ." They laugh together, realizing they
were both feeling the same way about their relationship,
but did not know how to talk about it or change it.

Keep your relationship from getting "stale" by sharing new activities together.

This couple realizes that many of the activities they
wanted to share with a fantasized new partner were actually
very similar, but they had neglected to discuss or share them
with one another. Although their midnight rendezvous had
begun as an effort to escape boredom by finding someone
new and exciting to share their lives with, they used this
occasion as the start of a "renewal" in their own relationship.

You might be surprised to discover that your mate has
very interesting dreams and desires that he or she would
love to experience with you; you are, after all, the person's
chosen companion. Most of us enjoy newness in our lives.
But, when a married person looks for newness in some*one*

rather than some*thing*, they could be setting themselves up for a fidelity pitfall. It makes more sense to explore new activities as a couple, instead of finding a new person to share them with.

During the course of mar-riage you might try doing things together, but sometimes fall into a rut and do the same things over and over. If a couple's night out consists of watching TV on Saturday night or going to dinner and a movie week after week after week, it's easy for the couple to feel that the mar-riage is becoming routine and stale. Yet, for a husband and wife to actually come up with—

> *Most of us enjoy "newness" in our lives. A fidelity pitfall can occur if a married person looks for this in some*one* new rather than some*thing* new.*

and then try out—new experiences might not be easy. Old habits can be hard to break, and some couples just aren't used to creative thinking in this aspect of their lives. Take heart: Try it, you may like it!

New experiences need not be exotic or expensive. Exploring the world together doesn't have to cost a lot of money. In terms of how it affects the quality of a marriage, partners can do just as well by going for drives or walks in new locations in their community or visiting local points of interest as they can by traveling halfway around the world or visiting a famous museum or shrine. Consider what Thoreau had to say about this in his essay on walking: "An absolutely new prospect is a great happiness, and I can still get this any afternoon. . . . Walking will carry me to as strange a country as I expect ever to see. A single farm-house which I had not seen before is sometimes as good as the dominions of [a] King . . ."

Many couples may have no interest in walking. That's okay; what counts is finding things to do or adventures to share that please the two of you. Look in your local paper for activities and find something that is free or inexpensive, or create your own: Visit a local factory; ask an artisan to show you how he creates beautiful objects of wood or glass; go to a concert in the park or a lecture on a topic of interest; visit several art galleries; take a hike or bike ride ending with a picnic; watch the sunset from a mountain top (or rooftop); the list of potentially interesting shared activities is limitless. All it really takes is a desire to discover or experience some facet of life together. Have you ever spent an evening watching a romantic movie and giving each other a full body massage with lotion? Not only is this very relaxing, it can be a delightful way to enhance intimacy.

Just Do It!

Be creative. Share with each other those things that you've always wanted to do, and determine which ones might be worth pursuing together. Or, simply follow through on a spontaneous "Gee, that sounds like fun!" idea. Just do it! Who knows? Some couples might get a thrill from blasting each other for a couple of hours at a paintball gallery, while others would enjoy listening to a string quartet at the local college. It doesn't really matter what you do together, just as long as you spend time sharing your life. Taking the initiative to plan shared activities is a delightful, appropriate way for each of you to implement "The Golden Rule" in your relationship. Besides providing opportunities to enjoy life together, it gives both mates a chance to understand and appreciate their partner more fully.

Another important reason for marriage partners to engage in new experiences is this: Because the activity is new to both of them, it helps them feel they are learning together and interacting on the same level, instead of in superior/subordinate roles, which can happen when either person has already had the experience and leads the way. The freshness of the new experience enhances the vitality of the relationship. For example, couples who have been married for many years and take up a new hobby together often experience a newness in their relationship, as this new, shared activity regenerates their feelings for each other.

Renewed Experiences

Although it's exciting to engage in new experiences together, equally important is remembering those things which brought you together in the first place. The beginning of your relationship was an exciting time—one filled with anticipation, excitement, and romance. Think back and remember those experiences—not only the activities, but the feelings you had with your companion. Those feelings grew and developed until you decided you wanted to spend the rest of your lives together. Make sure you create opportunities to duplicate not only the activities, but the emotions associated with those activities.

You might look back and think, "I wish I could feel that way again about him or her." You can, and it can be even better! Depending on where you are in your relationship, it may be fairly easy, or it may take many weeks of applying the practices outlined in this book, but it can happen; don't give up. Loving your companion is a decision you alone make, and one you need to renew every day. To love your mate is to live out your commitment to him or her. This requires a continual rededication of heart and mind to the relationship you have invested so much time and energy in. After all, this is the one person in the world whom you have chosen to be your prime companion throughout life!

So, when you plan to re-create the activity—whether it is going back to the place you spent your honeymoon or to the movie you saw together when you "fell in love"— remember to also put effort into generating the feelings of love,

> *Loving our chosen companion is a decision you make, and need to renew every day.*

excitement, and warmth you had with the original activity. There are some important things to remember to avoid disappointment in this process.

How many of us have gone away on a second honeymoon, remembering how "perfect," "romantic," and "exciting" the original honeymoon was? The sunset was the best you'd ever seen, the dinner was fantastic, and your sweet-heart looked great! When we try to re-create the experience, it somehow falls short. There are clouds in the sky blocking the sunset, the meat was overcooked at dinner, or your spouse may have put on twenty pounds. Not the same, right?

Right and wrong. It is different. Every experience in life is different, whether it's the physical surroundings that change or your feelings at the moment, perhaps due to other external factors. (If you just got a speeding ticket on the way to your hotel, it may take a while to get into a good mood again.) When we try to compare current experiences to previous ones, they tend to fall short of our expectations in some way. This happens for two reasons:

1. Memories refine themselves over time.
2. You and your companion are different people than you were. You've lived life longer, and shared more positive and negative experiences together.

Remember this about renewed experiences: The actual experiences we have are rarely as good as the memories which spring from them. The memory refines itself over time and often makes the event seem better than it actually was. Thus, when we try to re-create it, we may feel the renewed experience falls short of our memory. To avoid this, consider focusing on the special aspects of each event as you are experiencing it. In re-creating a special experience, allow this new event to generate its own unique emotions and memories. Make sure your expectation of the event is appropriate, and you'll not be as easily disappointed. Recognize that it will be different, and then enjoy the dif-ferences. Share the positive memories about the event and compare them to where you are now and how far you've come together. Laugh about it and smile when you remember the "good ol' days." Set new goals for your life. Celebrate the successes you've had together, no matter how small. It's the accumulation of small, shared experiences along the way that make a great marriage. Recognize these small successes for how significant they are.

Traditions are another part of renewed experiences in marriage. It's quite normal for many people to think about special family traditions, but less common for couples to develop and nurture special marriage traditions. Committed companions strive to cultivate some of their renewed shared experiences as special marriage traditions they look forward to again and again. Do you have any special marriage traditions? You may think you don't have any, but consider these examples, and then identify yours, or come up with some new ones of your own:

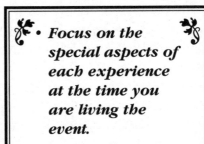

• Focus on the special aspects of each experience at the time you are living the event.

• In re-creating a special experience, allow this new event to generate its own unique feelings and memories.

- Watching romantic movies on Valentine's Day.
- On your partner's birthday, write a letter telling him or her some new ways you've come to love the person.
- On your wedding anniversary, eat waffles with strawberries and whipped cream in bed (or whatever you ate on your honeymoon).
- On New Year's Day, take time to review the year's accomplishments and your goals for the next year.

What About Time Apart?

If the essence of sharing is spending time together, what happens if you're in a situation that requires some periods of separation? There are times when our careers or other circumstances require that we spend time apart from one another. In today's complex world, it's quite realistic for practically any couple to anticipate that there may be at least some periods of separation from their mate. Limited separations are a part of life, and every couple can endure them.

Being apart need not be traumatic or damaging to the relationship, but does require that partners make appropriate adaptations. We spent several months in transition while preparing for professional opportunities in different states. So, we've had to learn to adjust to a "commuter marriage" with periods of separation. The key to surviving occasional or lengthy separations is mutual agreement, understanding, and commitment to each other. They are also easier to deal with when parameters are clearly defined and we know the separation has a limited time frame, or when there are periods between the separations when renewal of relationships can occur.

*S*USAN:

Recently, I was given an extra assignment at work, which required a significant investment of my time and energy. I immediately went home and talked with Tres about it. I told him what I thought it meant in terms of time away and the length of time involved to get the project under control. I knew I could get it under control and manageable in a three-month period. Thus, we both had an expectation that in three months things would return to "normal." We ensured we had at least a weekly night out, and spent time together grocery shopping, washing the car, and doing other activities usually done alone. We talked about key issues or concerns during these times and caught up on our personal experiences, feelings, goals, and so forth. At the end of three months, the workload was stabilized, and the extra time at work was not needed. If this had continued, we might have wanted to consider an alternative plan.

The process of life itself can also get in the way of sharing time together. There are so many things pulling at us and consuming our time, and we can become so busy with other legitimate aspects of life that our time with one another can get lost.

A husband found himself in a tough situation with his wife, who was continually working all hours of the day and night. They were both professionals, so he tried to be understanding. He never knew when she was going to be home, and he hated going home to an empty house. So he began delaying going home and finding excuses to go out to dinner with friends, go to the gym, or anything else to fill the time. After about a year of this, they realized that when they were together they were always fighting, and they did not like being together. Both realized they hardly knew each other anymore.

Here, expectations were not understood and the couple drifted apart as the two failed to recognize the significant impact these patterns had on their relationship—until it was too late. When we know there is something that is going to require a lot of our time, we need to define it and discuss how we can still ensure time for each other.

Sharing is one way we can find more happiness in our lives by recognizing and appreciating the "moments of joy" for ourselves and for our sweetheart.

MAIN IDEAS:
Share

- The essence of *Share* is to spend time with our chosen companion.
- Partners need to balance the time they spend at work, with others, and in personal pursuits with time they share with their mates.
- Convert some personal activities into those shared with your mate.
- Share more time doing ordinary activities that are a part of everyday life, including chores, errands, etc.
- Couples can find more time to share together by spending less time watching TV, which, even when viewed together, rarely leads to meaningful sharing.
- Sharing new experiences creates memories and keeps the relationship from getting stale.
- Create newness in your relationship by doing something new, not finding someone new.
- New experiences need not be exotic or expensive, simply different.
- Couples benefit when some new experiences require both partners to learn together as beginners.
- Renewed experiences help us remember and re-create the feelings that brought us together.
- With renewed experiences, remember that memories refine themselves over time; you're different people, and every experience is different, so don't get caught in feeling the renewed activity is not as good as the original one.
- Loving your mate is a decision you make every day.
- Make your shared moments of joy more tangible by recognizing and discussing your feelings with each other.

20 QUESTIONS
to Ponder and Discuss

First, ask yourself the following questions about how you share life with your companion. Then, discuss them with your companion by asking: "How am I doing?" and "How might we improve?"

1. Do we realize that it's only when we spend time together that we can actually interact and engage in the activities that make a relationship a thriving one?
2. Am I as eager to spend time with my partner as I am with others or in personal pursuits?
3. Are there some activities I enjoy, but prefer not to share with my partner? Does he or she understand and accept my reasons for this preference?
4. Could some of my personal interests and enjoyable activities become ones that we share together?
5. Have we brainstormed recently to identify the kinds of experiences we'd like to share together?
6. What can we do together tonight instead of watching TV or a video?
7. Is it possible for us to carry out some daily tasks, errands, or projects together that would help us spend more meaningful time as a couple?
8. Are there certain responsibilities we've previously done separately or considered part of our partner's role that we might benefit by doing jointly?
9. Do my spouse and I enjoy sharing new activities together? Am I willing to explore new areas with my partner?
10. What hobby or interest might we enjoy that would be completely new to both of us?
11. Is there a place neither of us has ever been that we'd enjoy?

12. Do I frequently look for ways to surprise my mate? When was the last time we did something together that was totally spontaneous?
13. What can we do to laugh and smile more? Should we spend more time with others who are good-natured?
14. Do I recognize and appreciate the feelings that are generated as we share new experiences now?
15. Do I have fun with my mate? Do I know what he or she likes to do for fun? What can we do to have more fun?
16. What shared activities that were special to both of us can we continue to renew as cherished traditions?
17. Are there things we used to do together that we haven't done in a long time, that we might enjoy doing again?
18. Do I do romantic things the way I did in the beginning of our relationship (send love notes, give flowers, call for a lunch date, etc.)?
19. Do I remember and seek to renew the special feelings I had for my sweetheart when we were dating?
20. What else have we learned about the *Share* practice (outside of this book) that we can apply to our benefit?

Now What?

After answering the questions and discussing your individual areas of need, review the ideas we've included as examples of things you can do to begin sharing more time together. Use the *KISS Marriage Maker*™ to establish your goals for new and renewed experiences with your companion as frequently as possible. This can be a surprise you plan for your mate, or something developed together as you both decide what you'd like to do. Some activities take time to plan or re-create; others can be done on the spur of the moment with virtually no advance planning.

SHARE:
Ideas to Consider

The following list of ideas may be a place to start as you determine specific things you will do to share both new and renewed experiences with your companion:

- Watch a sunset (or "people-watch" at a mall or airport).
- Go for a scenic drive (mountains, ocean, etc.).
- Learn a foreign language (maybe even "signing").
- Go to an athletic event (besides your kids' soccer game).
- Give each other a backrub with lotion or baby oil.
- Cook a meal (try cuisine from Hungary or Ethiopia).
- Visit an art gallery (free cheese and crackers are a bonus!).
- Take a college or adult education class.
- Go to a play or concert (even at your kids' school).
- Walk along the beach (or at a local park or playground).
- Go snowshoeing or cross-country skiing.
- Take dancing lessons (try the "Tango" or "Two-Step").
- Take a trip to someplace new (even short day-trips).
- Go rock-climbing, white-river rafting, or four-wheeling.
- Read and discuss a book or article (starting with this one!).
- Watch races (motor-cross, power boats, or stock cars).
- Play co-ed softball (on the same team!).
- Take up a new hobby (anything will do).
- Build a bathroom (or less ambitious—a garden patio).
- Learn to play musical instruments (even the washboard).
- Watch a foreign video.
- Join a club or organization.
- Go dancing. (Yes! This is one of the best!)

"A true friend unbosoms freely, advises justly, assists readily, adventures boldly, takes all patiently, defends courageously, and continues a friend unchangeably."

— *William Penn* —

CARE

*Nurture a Best-Friends Relationship
with Your Husband or Wife*

$\mathcal{R}$EMEMBER the very best friend you ever had? Think about that relationship. What did you do together? Everything? You could talk about anything, right? Did you worry if he or she was going to judge you? Criticize you? Accept you with the good and bad traits you have? Did you trust the person's opinion? Have respect for the person? Listen to his or her ideas? Did you ever get mad at each other? Did you make up? Did the person say and do things to make you feel better about yourself? Did you take turns being first? Share? Did you understand him or her—how the person was going to act or react—but loved and accepted each other anyway?

At some point in our lives, most of us have had a "best friend" like this—someone we confided our innermost secrets, dreams, and goals to. Usually, this was an individual with whom we felt free to discuss every topic imaginable, because we trusted the person not to violate our confidences. Another reason we felt safe and comfortable is because he or she accepted us for who we were—in spite of all our shortcomings—instead of having our friendship based on conditions or expectations.

What value did you place on this friendship and this person? Did you want to make sure you didn't lose such a friend? Would you carefully consider your actions, thoughts, and their feelings with whatever you did? Of course.

As children and teenagers, our best friends were usually individuals of our own gender, but as we grew older and the nature of our associations and relationships changed, our best friends often became persons of the opposite sex. Some individuals are fortunate when they get married to feel they have married their very best friend.

Then, what happens over time? Why do we sometimes feel different or not value this relationship with our spouse as much? As a relationship persists, some people begin to take their partners for granted, assuming, "They'll always be here . . . we're married!"

Regardless of where you are now, most of us would like to feel that the person we spend a lifetime with is, indeed, our very best friend. There are many ways we can cultivate genuine friendships with others. Remember, if we expect our mate to be our best friend, we need to be a best friend for our mate. We've identified six keys essential in developing and maintaining a best-friends relationship:

Acceptance	Commitment
Understanding	Affirmation
Respect	Support

Of all six practices, *Care* is most closely related to what many consider "love." Genuine love is related to serving others. As we care for one another in the ways discussed in this chapter, our sincere service will increase our feelings of mutual love. So you'll find that your efforts to accept, understand, respect, commit, affirm, and support your mate will yield great dividends. Both of you will reap the reward of a lifetime of positive experiences filled with joy and warm memories with a companion you truly enjoy sharing your life with. The following is a brief discussion about some important aspects of these crucial ways to care for your husband or wife as your very "best friend" on earth.

Acceptance

Husbands and wives need to truly accept their mates just as they are, and not condition their acceptance on their spouses becoming as they would like them to be. One problem plaguing many marriages occurs when one spouse tries to change or improve his or her mate. Even if the intention in doing this is positive, the outcome is almost always disastrous.

If we truly feel we have a best friend in our spouse, we're usually more willing to listen to his or her feedback about our attitudes or behaviors. We don't become easily offended when input is offered with the love and kindness of a sensitive friend. After all, best friends should be able to both give and receive constructive criticism from one another.

A time-tested piece of advice often given to couples during their courtship may be useful for couples already married: "Keep your eyes wide open before marriage and half-closed afterwards." In other words, the prime time to carefully scrutinize and evaluate

> **"Keep your eyes wide open before marriage and half-closed afterwards."**

a potential marriage partner is before making the decision to marry him or her. Once that decision has been made, what's called for is a very high level of tolerance and patience. Every person has numerous flaws and shortcomings, and the longer we are married to someone, the more aware of these we become. The truth is, if we primarily were to evaluate our spouses based on their personal weaknesses, every married person alive could find numerous reasons to end their marriage! But, if we want to sincerely care for our partners, we need to frequently remind ourselves—and them—that we accept them just as they are.

RES:

Throughout my life, I've had numerous opportunities to be around my father as he interacted with others, both professionally and socially. He has always been extremely gregarious, and frequently took the initiative to give "unsolicited advice" to almost anybody in a rather light-hearted, good-natured way. This came quite naturally, as his profession was a motivational speaker and psychologist.

The one piece of advice which he gave most often—I'm certain I heard him say this hundreds of times—was this: "Be kind to your wife."

At the time—particularly when I was a teenager—I remember thinking this was rather presumptuous of him to be telling others what to do in their marriages. Yet, as I've reflected on this during my adult years, I've come to the conclusion that this simple counsel to be kind to our mates is perhaps one of the single most important reminders every marriage partner needs. What better way is there to show that we truly care for our beloved wife or husband than to treat her or him with kindness?

Obviously, there are some qualities or behaviors in our mates that we do not want to accept, which need to change in order for us to feel satisfied with our marriage. Nevertheless, it's important to recognize that for a spouse to even want to change, he or she needs to feel that, overall, we accept them for who they are. As individuals, we should always improve ourselves and work to overcome our bad habits. This is easier to do with the support and love of our "best friends." (Chapter 5, *Confront,* and Chapter 6, *Resolve,* cover the principles and practices couples can apply to help achieve change in their relationships.)

Understanding

How often do you ask yourself: "Who is this person I love, and what is important to him or her?" and "Has that changed?"

*T*RES:

I have never forgotten one textbook which stood out among all those that I was required to read in graduate school. It was a very skinny book (maybe

that's why I remember it!) written by a Swiss psychi-
atrist, Paul Tournier, entitled *To Understand Each
Other.* I remember feeling at that time—and have
come to appreciate even more deeply during these
last 25 years—that, in some respects, this simple yet
powerful idea, "to understand each other," is the real
essence of healthy marriages. Husbands and wives
who desire to nurture a "best-friends" relationship
would do well to remember this.

In order to understand our husbands or wives, we need
to learn as much as we can about them. This includes
appreciating feelings, aspirations, hopes, fears, sources of
pleasure and joy, and knowing their opinions about important issues. Because every individual continually changes
over time, we need to keep up the habit of engaging in
meaningful conversations with our mate. By asking
thoughtful questions and listening carefully, we can
expand our awareness, sensitivity, and appreciation for the
person our mate is becoming. "To understand each other"
is an ongoing process in marriage—not a static condition
spouses arrive at.

Respect
In order to care for our best friend, we need to respect
him or her as a valued individual. You might ask yourself:
"What is respect?" "How do I know whether my behavior
toward my mate conveys genuine respect?" "How can I
show greater respect for my beloved companion?"

Three definitions of respect from Webster's Dictionary
can help us answer these questions and apply this principle in our marriage relationships:

1. "To consider worthy of high regard or
   esteem."
2. "To give particular attention to . . ."
3. "To refrain from interfering with . . ."

"To consider worthy of high regard or esteem"

Every person on the planet is of immense value, simply because they exist. All are unique individuals with their own distinctive sets of experiences, talents, strengths, and perspectives, and thus deserve a fundamental respect, even before they've "earned" it. If we respect all persons because of their inherent value, how much more should we respect that person we have chosen as our lifelong companion?

Marriage partners who genuinely respect each other do not swear, use foul language or put each other down. On the contrary, in nurturing respect, you will go out of your way to be especially courteous and kind to this person. Even when you think that your name-calling is "just for fun" or your sarcasm is done in a joking manner, your mate may not be feeling anything but the unkind words that are said and may never receive them with humor. Even when used to express your strong feelings, swearing or any kind of foul language is disrespectful. Furthermore, it usually turns people off and they don't listen to what you have to say. Unfortunately, most spouses are quite unaware when they communicate a lack of respect toward their mates.

Nevertheless, this is one bad habit, even if subconscious, that deserves our concerted efforts and commitment to recognize and change. For those of you on the receiving end of this type of behavior, it is critical that you assume personal responsibility to assist your partner in recognizing when he or she has said something that offends or hurts you. To effectively eliminate a habit like this requires feedback every single time the person slips into disrespectful communication. Both partners need to give and receive feedback, in the spirit of love, when this occurs and commit to making their relationship a better one.

*T*RES:

A couple came to me with this problem: Mary was feeling verbally abused, but Carl did not realize the things he was saying were mean and hurtful. He said pretty much everything that came to mind with complete disregard for others' sensitivity. Although Carl did swear, his problem was not so much the use of foul language as it was talking to everyone—including Mary—sarcastically and using cutting remarks. Carl's verbally abusive outbursts were so frequent and offensive that they even angered and embarrassed any family members who happened to be around.

This tore at Mary's sense of self-worth and made it hard for her to feel loving toward him. When we discussed it, Carl said he had no intention of being hurtful, but that this was a long-time habit he had developed growing up in his family. He expressed a desire to change his habits but said he needed help. I asked Carl what Mary might say or do to cue him when he was being inappropriate. He indicated several things for her not to say or do, since whenever she did them, they only made him mad. He then decided on a cue word she could say that would help him notice his bad language but not result in an angry reaction on his part. He also agreed to apologize and give her a hug to show he was trying to be more sensitive and caring. Both were surprised how quickly Carl changed his habit, and the way this sensitivity and respect increased their sense of feeling like friends.

Here are some ways to restore a sense of regard and esteem for one another:

1. Acknowledge there is a problem in this area.
2. Discuss the problem using specific examples. (See guidelines in *Confront* and *Resolve* chapters.)
3. Agree on a plan of action that reminds one mate if he or she slips back into old habits.

Done properly, this is an effective way to care as best friends and grow together. If you have problems dealing with this kind of challenge on your own, you may wish to seek help from a skilled professional counselor.

"To give particular attention to"

Living in this fast-paced, complex world makes it very easy for partners to take their spouses for granted. But we need to show our mates respect by paying attention to them as valued individuals facing continual pressures. Although unintentional, taking anyone for granted significantly diminishes the respect in a couple's relationship and can even lead to indifference.

One way to counteract these habits is to reflect on how your life would be different without your companion—as a breadwinner, a lover, a friend, your partner in parenting, one who helps prepare the meals or fixes things around the house, and so on. As your partner in marriage, the person plays many roles, and his or her efforts to do so deserve both your appreciation and respect.

Another element of respect is that which is earned. We respect people for many different reasons, all of which are either internally or externally driven. Here's the problem: In our success-oriented culture, we tend to feel that those who deserve our respect have earned it because of external factors—what they have achieved or acquired, their wealth, occupation, car, clothes, house, and so on. But this societal tendency can create problems in marriage. If the respect we show our mate is based primarily upon these external factors, then our respect will fluctuate with the inevitable changes in external circumstances. Such changes may have very little to do with who our husband or wife really is. Ask yourself, "Is my husband more worthy of respect because of the expensive car he just acquired, or less worthy because he's going bald or got laid off in a company downsizing? Do I respect my wife more because of her raise or less because she lost a breast in a mastectomy?"

> *Respect should be based primarily on internal qualities rather than on external factors.*

These changes that occur in life are why we should base our

respect for our spouses upon internal factors, such as the values and principles they practice in their daily lives and the way they treat others. The consistency with which our spouses conduct their personal lives, in spite of continuous external changes, is a better indicator of the respect we should give them than the changes themselves.

In reality, each person is multifaceted. We will all feel better about ourselves if at least our spouse recognizes and respects our efforts to develop as a balanced person. So, in addition to paying attention to our mate's temporal growth (which is externally based), marriage partners should also focus on their companion's emotional, social and spiritual growth, which tends to be related to internal factors and reflects more of who they really are. Therefore, spouses show wisdom when they base their respect for each other on internal factors—such as how they handle adversity or the compassion they show others. Husbands and wives do well to respect each other more for their integrity than for their income, more for their goodness than for their good looks.

It is important to take a closer look at why you respect your spouse. This is an important question to ask, especially if you are feeling a lack of respect for your sweetheart. Why?

A middle-aged friend's husband recently lost his executive level job. His ego and self-esteem suffered as he tried to redefine who he was. He had always viewed himself as a successful businessman who supported his family very well. He was now unemployed, could not find a job, and began to lose self-respect. His wife lost what she defined as respect for him because he could no longer support the family. Both had defined respect based on external factors. Yet, he was the same person with the same beliefs, values, and qualities. Yes, they had suffered a loss. But what had been lost was some measure of economic stability, not the essence of who he was.

Would you consider losing respect for your neighbor because he lost his job due to a company downsizing? Typically, we are more understanding and respectful toward others than we are toward our own companions.

*O*RES:

In counseling with a couple, it was clear that the wife was struggling with what she identified as a loss of respect for her husband because he was very poor at managing their family finances. She was continually frustrated, as bills weren't paid and their money was sometimes spent unwisely.

My counsel to her was: "Instead of allowing your feelings of disrespect toward your husband to grow and fester, why not consider a different approach? By discussing this matter together, perhaps you can both simply acknowledge that financial management is not one of his strengths. Therefore, why not decide to let you be the 'money manager' of the family? This way, you can begin to focus your perceptions and feelings on his areas of strength."

"To refrain from interfering with"

It's easy to fall into the trap of treating a spouse the way we treat our children. This can take such forms as nagging, scolding, or using force with our mates. All are attempts to exert control, and all are inappropriate. One reason we can unwittingly show disrespect for our marriage partner is that parental responsibilities sometimes require us to be directive in defining what our children may or may not do. This can also be reinforced if our job calls for us to take charge of those with whom we work.

To avoid this problem, we need to differentiate our marital roles from our parental or vocational roles, and continually remind ourselves that it is inappropriate to be directive with our spouse. What's appropriate is to show great respect for our spouses as adults with the inalienable right to exercise their own agency. We should grant our partners the respect to make decisions about how they will behave and how they will choose to live their lives.

Commitment

When a man and woman commit themselves to each other upon making their marriage vows, they both pledge to be loyal and faithful to this companion regardless of the challenges of life. "In sickness and in health" and "for richer or for poorer" are the standard lines.

Far too often in today's world, when the going gets tough, the weak get going! In other words, noncommitted companions simply move out and move on all too readily. We live in a disposable society, not only of goods and services, but also of relationships. We feel we need to get rid of or run away from the problems we encounter. Naturally, we are all aware of situations in which getting out of a marriage is the only healthy alternative, but too many couples give up on a marriage when what they need to do is reaffirm their commitment to each other, and then work to get through the tough stuff so they will emerge with a stronger relationship. It can—and does—happen all the time.

𝒮USAN:

I remember after I had left home and married, my mother considered getting a divorce. She and my dad had fought for years and did not seem to have very much in common anymore, much less a "best-friends" relationship. My brother was a junior in high school at the time, and when Mom talked with him about her feelings, he asked her not to leave him and his dad. His pleas made such an impact that she made a decision at that point to "stick it out" for her son. This turned out to be the right decision. Not only did she "stick it out" through the tough times, but what emerged was a stronger relationship and greater love between her and my dad than they had ever experienced before. As they grew older, with the children grown and gone, she developed a serious, eventually terminal illness which required my father to care for her with increasing intensity as the years went by. He grew to love her more with each day of service and care, and she grew to love him more because of his love, caring, and com-

mitment to her. He remained committed to her to the
end—and misses her dearly since her passing. She told
me several months before her death that the decision
she made to stay with him and love him was the best
one she could have made, and that her love and commitment for him only grew more intense and mature
with the passing years. She died with a special love for
him that would never have developed except for the
trials they endured together.

At the core of maintaining your sense of commitment
and loyalty to your marriage partner is absolute fidelity—
maintaining the exclusivity of your sexual relationship with
each other. Furthermore, those who are "committed to
remaining committed" to their mate will use wisdom and
discretion in the ways that they not only interact with, but
also think about, other individuals of the opposite sex.
Although allowing yourself to dream about sexual fantasies
with others might seem harmless, this practice can easily
plant the seed of infidelity.

Affirmation

There's certainly a place for competition in life, but not
for couples in a thriving marriage. After all, our journey on
the Marriage Highway is not a road race, but the opportunity for partners to enjoy one another's company along the
way. It's unfortunate when life partners try to compete
with, and even feel threatened by, their mates. Marriages
thrive when both husband and wife make it a point to let
each other know they're truly delighted with one another's
accomplishments and successes. Rejoicing in others' successes is the hallmark of a person who is a great friend and
personally mature.

A primary reason people marry in the first place is that
the man or woman they've chosen brings out the best in
them more than most people they know. We should make
it a high priority to continually bring out the best in our
companions and celebrate each other's successes together.

Here are things you might say to affirm your mate:
- "I'm very confident in you."
- "You did a terrific job!"
- "Thanks for all you do to make my life better."
- "I'm so grateful you're my wife; there's no one in all the world I'd rather share my life with!"
- "Besides being so capable, you are so good. I'm very blessed that you're my husband!"

Everyone needs to be encouraged and appreciated. Try to think of different ways to affirm your sweetheart through sincere, positive expressions or terms of endearment.

Support

Every person sometimes falls short or blatantly fails in his or her endeavors. Therefore, best friends not only delight in their mate's successes, but are willing to support them during "down" times. Even the most optimistic people get discouraged with or disappointed in themselves. Trying to cheer up your spouse or offering a word of encouragement can do wonders. Listening empathically and helping your companion sort through feelings to regain a positive perspective are effective ways to be supportive.

Sometimes the troubles we encounter call for more than an empathetic ear or words of encouragement. If you truly desire to be your mate's best friend, offer to lend a helping hand. Make it a point to ask not only open-ended, "How can I help?" questions, but to offer your help in specific ways. For example, if your wife seems a bit stressed in preparing for a presentation, you might ask, "Would it help you concentrate better if I fix dinner, clean up the dishes, and put the kids to bed?" Other times it's best to take the initiative and do whatever seems to help without asking or being told.

Many individuals believe that the best way to support others is

The Platinum Rule:

Do unto your mate as your mate would have you do unto him or her.

by living The Golden Rule: "Do unto others as you would have them do unto you." Although well-intentioned, there is a higher principle that's especially useful as you attempt to support your marriage partner. For many years, family experts have referred to this higher principle—which is more valuable—as *The Platinum Rule*: "Do unto your mate as *your mate* would have you do unto him or her."

Susan:

> A perfect example of this in our own marriage is a simple backrub. When I give Tres a backrub, he generally likes it firm and hard—to knead his muscles with real vigor. On the other hand, when he gives me a backrub, I generally prefer a soft, gentle touch that barely skims the surface of the skin. To me, this kind of backrub is far more relaxing and comforting than a vigorous massage. The point is, we both need to take our cues from each other—rather than using our own preferences—in trying to be supportive of one another. (Nevertheless, because I occasionally enjoy a firm massage to relieve my tense muscles and stress after a busy day, it's important for me to clearly express my preference at the time I ask—or he offers—to give me one of these oh-so-appreciated gifts.)

In other words, to truly support his wife, a husband uses what his wife desires as his frame of reference. Likewise, supportive wives will take their cues from their husband's wishes.

What If You're Currently Not Best Friends?

If you started out your marriage as best friends, but that has changed over time, you may want to spend more time on this section and review what has happened and why. Perhaps you found yourself reacting to difficult situations instead of treating each other in thoughtful, constructive ways. Maybe your feelings were hurt, and you built walls to protect your heart from further attack. ("Heart attacks" from a partner can be just as damaging to your emotional well-being as cardiac arrests can be to your physical health.) When this happens it can destroy feelings of respect and diminish a sense of acceptance, understanding, or support from your marriage partner.

*S*USAN:

A friend described the events leading to the destruction of her marriage this way:

"I had built a wall between my husband and me during years of feeling demeaned from his verbal abuse. I built the wall around my heart, for it had been badly hurt. My self-esteem was so diminished I could no longer 'absorb' within myself the negative remarks my husband so frequently made. He had resorted to so much name-calling and so many put-downs, I could hardly bear to be around him. He would ask my opinion about something, and I would answer, giving details and reasons why I felt the way I did. His response was: 'Well, that was a dumb thing to say' or 'I can't believe how stupid you are.' I finally developed the attitude of 'I'm not going to express my opinions anymore, because he obviously does not respect me.' Verbally and emotionally, I closed up to him. The wall was so high and so thick, I didn't know how to bring it down, even if he did change. Finally, our relationship ended in divorce."

Over the years, this pattern of protecting your heart can build a wall as large and formidable as that in Berlin, and just as difficult to get past. But, just like the Berlin Wall came down, so can the walls spouses have built to protect themselves from being hurt. Such walls can be taken down, one brick at a time, sometimes with a simple "I'm sorry. I didn't mean to hurt your feelings. Will you please forgive me?" It takes both people realizing what has happened and being willing to change their behaviors, as well as their responses to each other. Habits are hard to break, but it's easier if we deal with them as early as possible. We review ways to constructively bring up sensitive issues in the *Confront* chapter, and offer guidelines for effectively solving problems in the *Resolve* chapter.

> *Caring is an attitude followed by actions . . .*
>
> *Decide to care about your companion and then do something about it!*

In similar fashion, positive connecting links—bridges between each other's heart—can also be rebuilt, one brick at a time, with each caring moment, every sensitive comment, or any considerate action we use in relating to our spouse with genuine caring. What's needed is a commitment to clear the slate, start fresh, and begin again to trust and open your heart to your companion. This new beginning can commence when either spouse shows the humility and maturity to express a sincere apology.

The bridge-building referred to above illustrates a most valuable consequence that happens as a partner strives to sincerely care for his or her mate. Partners who cultivate the *Care* practice find that they automatically reinforce a quality necessary in all solid relationships: trust. With each principle we apply to show that we care, we are also developing a relationship built on deeper levels of trust. To accept our partner as he or she is means we trust that he or she is capable of changing in a climate of patience and tolerance. Seeking to really understand this person signifies that we trust the person to be one worth knowing better, regardless of any quirks, feelings, or struggles he or she may have. Trust is an obvious prerequisite to respecting our partner's right to make his or her own choices. We must trust our mate in order to make a serious commitment and dedication to each other and to our relationship. Similarly, it's difficult to affirm or support our mate unless we trust that he or she will accept our sincere expressions of heartfelt emotions. Thus, as we learn to consistently and effectively care for our mate, we are also developing the deeper levels of trust necessary to connect with our soulmate in both emotional and physical intimacy.

Because trust is so important in our relationship, it should be guarded and protected. But, once broken, recognize that it will take significant energy, time, and commitment to restore. This is especially true if the violated trust involves infidelity.

So, what if you feel your trust has been destroyed? How do you rebuild it? Here's a place to start:

1. With a sincere apology by the one who has broken the trust.
2. Forgiveness and a willingness to allow your mate the opportunity to earn your trust again.
3. By one action at a time, over time. Discuss together what is expected from the "trust breaker" that will help to rebuild it. (Example: Calling if you're going to be later than planned, agreeing to not spend money from the joint account unless agreed upon, not flirting with others at the workplace, following through on promises, etc.)

Time is the healing element, and trust can be rebuilt when proven over time. (To do this effectively, some couples may need to seek professional assistance.)

Developing and maintaining a best-friends relationship helps us know there is one person we can always count on. This reinforces our sense of security, inner peace, and comfort in an otherwise unstable world. Having this com-

> *Marriage relationships can be rebuilt one brick at a time— one caring moment, one sensitive comment, or one considerate action at a time.*

panionship helps us experience the joy of a rich, fulfilled life which comes from practicing the values of acceptance, understanding, respect, commitment, affirmation and support.

Caring is an attitude followed by actions. Decide to care about your companion, and then *do* something about it! Be your spouse's very best friend.

MAIN IDEAS:
Care

Six ways to develop a "best-friends" relationship with your husband or wife:

1. *Acceptance*—Embrace your spouse willingly and patiently, as he or she is.

2. *Understanding*—Seek to know and appreciate each other completely and empathically.

3. *Respect*—Treat each other with courtesy, attentiveness, and tolerance.

4. *Commitment*—Demonstrate loyalty through persistent perseverance and total fidelity.

5. *Affirmation*—Bring out the best in each other and celebrate successes together.

6. *Support*—Be there when and how your mate needs you, with words and actions.

Caring is an attitude followed by actions. Decide to care about your companion, then do something about it!

20 QUESTIONS
to Ponder and Discuss

First ask yourself the following questions about how you care for your husband or wife. Then discuss the questions with your husband or wife by asking: "How am I doing?" and "How might we improve?"

1. Do I actually feel that my spouse is my very best friend?
2. Do I care for my mate in a way that helps him or her feel I am a best friend?
3. How accepting am I of my spouse, even though I'm more aware of his of her flaws than anyone else?
4. What changes might I make that would improve my acceptance of my spouse?
5. How well do I know and understand my mate?
6. Do our conversations focus on helping me understand my spouse's opinions and feelings?
7. Do I ask questions to increase my awareness, sensitivity, and appreciation for my marriage partner as a person?
8. Do I treat my spouse with dignity, courtesy, and kindness?
9. Do I pay sufficient attention to my spouse so that he or she feels respected?
10. Is my respect for my spouse driven by internal or external factors?
11. Do I honor my partner in exercising his or her agency to make choices?
12. How strong is my commitment to my partner and to our relationship?
13. Am I willing to persevere in working through challenges with my spouse?
14. Do my actions, thoughts, and feelings reinforce my commitment to being completely faithful to my soulmate?
15. Do I rejoice in my spouse's successes?
16. Do I actively seek out opportunities to affirm my spouse by expressing positive feelings to him or her?

17. Am I there for my spouse, especially during his or her "down" times?
18. Do I know the ways in which my spouse prefers that I support him or her? Do I apply the Platinum Rule and ask my spouse what he or she wants?
19. What additional things can I do to show how much I care for my spouse?
20. What else have we learned about the *Care* practice (not from this book) that we can apply to our benefit?

Now What?

After evaluating where you are in the *Care* practice by answering the questions, review the applications and use the *KISS Marriage Maker*™ to set goals to improve those areas that need help. You might want to concentrate on one area for a week or two, then move on to another area. This is an effective way to specifically improve and see the results of your efforts.

CARE:
Ideas to Consider

The following ideas may be a place to start determining specific things you will do to show you care for your husband or wife:

- When watching the evening news and something interesting comes on, ask your spouse how he or she feels about it.
- Tell your companion at least one reason you respect him or her.
- Ask your spouse how you can support him or her at home, with children and relatives, work, and so forth.
- Be the first one to say "I'm sorry" when there's a misunderstanding.
- Tell your husband or wife, "Thank you for being my very best friend in the whole world!"
- Ask your mate how he or she feels about something going on in your life (career, kids in school, a child "leaving the nest," starting a new hobby, and so forth).
- Share with your partner something specific you appreciate about the kind of person he or she is.
- Ask your spouse how you can show your respect for him or her.
- Clean or polish your partner's running or dress shoes.
- Tell a friend or co-worker something you appreciate about your companion.
- Write a note to your in-laws expressing several of your mate's qualities you've come to value.
- Say to your spouse: "That's an interesting opinion. I'd like to know how you came to that conclusion."
- Express to your companion your willingness to see a problem through to its resolution. ("This matter is so important, I'm willing to take the morning off work to discuss and resolve it.")

- Take over one of your spouse's chores around the house for a day or week.
- Help your spouse with a special problem, project, goal, or dream; ask your spouse how you can best help.
- Express your awareness and acceptance of one of your mate's shortcomings in a good-natured way. ("Once I decipher your handwriting, I can see you have some great ideas!")
- The next time you notice an attractive person of the opposite sex, remind yourself of ways your own spouse appeals to you.

"How do I love thee? Let me count the ways. I love thee to the depth and breadth and height my soul can reach . . ."

— *Elizabeth Barrett Browning* —

CONNECT

Enhance the Emotional and
Physical Intimacy
with Your Soulmate

ℐT'S A tremendous blessing when a man and woman feel they have developed a "best-friends" relationship by cultivating the practice of caring for each other. Being best friends indicates there is some connecting going on—at least at a minimal level. Opening hearts and sharing feelings is the ultimate in emotional intimacy, so there is a natural progression and expansion from this phase of the relationship to the emotional and physical intimacy experienced by couples who make the marriage commitment.

Why do we use the expression "soulmate" in referring to the *Connect* practice in marriage? One definition of soul is "the union of a person's spirit with his or her body." Our spiritual nature actually encompasses our emotions, so "soulmates" refers to marriage partners who "mate" or "connect" on a spiritual, emotional, and physical level. This chapter will help couples strengthen their bond and deepen their joy by enhancing their connections in both the emotional and physical arenas of marriage.

Intimacy in marriage occurs when soulmates feel a sense of closeness and connection with each other. Intimacy has two components—emotional and physical. Although it's possible for spouses to experience physical intimacy without emotional intimacy, or emotional intimacy without physical intimacy, thriving couples need to connect on both levels.

Emotional Intimacy

There are many ways to cultivate emotional intimacy between husbands and wives. One way is to remember, rekindle, and build upon the feelings of closeness that brought you together. Perhaps the most important prerequisite for reinforcing such feelings is learning to share them openly with one another.

One of the first books that described this process was John Powell's *The Secret of Staying in Love*. Powell not only shows why sharing feelings is critical to emotional intimacy, but offers practical suggestions on how couples can implement this practice. Some of the most successful marriage enrichment programs are based on helping couples rekindle loving emotions and learn how to express their feelings to each other.

Marriage partners who want the satisfaction of an emotionally intimate relationship must open their hearts and share their innermost feelings with each other. This can be done through verbal dialogue, love letters, personal messages recorded on audio or video tape, and the like.

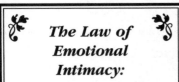

The Law of Emotional Intimacy:

"It's impossible to be emotionally intimate without being emotionally vulnerable."

We increase our feelings of closeness when we allow our spouse to know who we really are. This means eliminating any protective barriers and making ourselves as transparent as possible. Exposing oneself on a deep, emotional level is difficult for many people who have had their feelings hurt or have been previously "burned." Although remaining emotionally aloof is understandable, couples who are committed to a thriving marriage need to understand what I have defined as the *Law of Emotional Intimacy*. It's impossible to develop emotional intimacy without being emotionally vulnerable.

*O*RES:

One of the most pervasive trends since the 1970s is people's reluctance to make commitments in close relationships with the opposite sex. My experiences as a university professor and professional counselor have provided me a special window into the minds, hearts, and lifestyles of adults. I've observed that the societal tendency for low commitment among adults is strongly influenced by their unwillingness or inability to be emotionally vulnerable.

Unfortunately, individuals who have been emotionally aloof in their single life often have a hard time opening up to their marriage partners. Although each person is entitled to live his or her life as the person sees fit, as long as the person remains emotionally aloof to keep from getting hurt, he or she will inevitably experience the consequence of such action—a life characterized by superficial relationships, isolation, and loneliness.

Once individuals understand *The Law of Emotional Intimacy* and are determined to experience true intimacy in their relationships, they are ready to take the necessary risks of gaining it. Feeling close and staying connected with one's soulmate in a fragmented world is a prize well worth the price paid.

The good news is that every couple has the potential for an emotionally intimate marriage, regardless of reasons that may have reinforced a more guarded, less satisfying pattern in their interaction. Survivors of sexual abuse, adult children of dysfunctional families, individuals with shy or introverted personalities, and individuals whose trust has been exploited in previous relationships are all capable of connecting with their marriage partners in ways that are emotionally gratifying. As with most weaknesses in relationships, what's needed is an understanding of the correct principles and practices, and then the learning of how to apply these practices in your own life.

If I'm not comfortable expressing my thoughts and feelings, how do I begin? Here's a place to start:

1. Begin by admitting to your companion that this is an area you're uncomfortable with.
2. Ask for your companion's help, support, and understanding as you grow in this area.
3. Define what your best friend can do to help you feel more safe and comfortable sharing the feelings inside you. (Example: "When I tell you what I'm thinking or feeling, please don't criticize or laugh. Accept my ideas and emotions as where I am right now.")
4. Start with "baby steps." Share a little and see how it feels. Then, add more until you can share the deeper thoughts and feelings you have and feel safe.

> *Feeling close and staying connected with your soulmate in a fragmented world is a prize well worth the price paid.*

Most individuals thrive on the emotional intimacy they share with their soulmates and find this part of connecting a dimension which brings great satisfaction and significantly enhances the entire intimacy experience. This is one principle that, when practiced, can generate and cultivate immense joy within your soul. As you have quality experiences sharing on this intimate level, the bond between you grows even stronger. This deepens your inner peace and comfort, and thus contributes to a higher level of true marital joy. There is a stereotypical belief that women require more of an emotional connection in their sexual encounters than men, and that men do not want or feel much need for emotional intimacy. Although there may be some innate differences between men and women, most personality traits have nothing to do with gender. Everyone differs in their individual needs for emotional intimacy, both in quantity and quality. For some, less frequent but high-quality experiences in connecting are sufficient. Others may need to have much more frequent experiences with physical intimacy in order to even feel that they have connected emotionally, such as simple cuddling, looking into each other's eyes during lovemaking, or gentle caressing and talking with or without intercourse.

One of the reasons it is difficult for some men to be emotionally intimate is that they may not have taken the time to understand themselves, what they feel, and what their emotional needs really are. They clearly understand their physical needs, but tend to push their emotional ones aside, not realizing their importance in the relationship, much less for themselves as individuals. In general, women tend to take more time than men to recognize their feelings and determine what they need.

It is important to understand your own personal needs and wants and be able to communicate them to your spouse as clearly as possible: "I need to be held," "I want to see through your eyes into your heart," or "I would love to hear you tell me your deepest thoughts and dreams." It's impossible for our mates to meet our needs if they do not know what to do or how to do it. We need to define it for them. As we define our needs to our companions, they also should tell us what they need, and we should both be willing to respond accordingly.

There may be seminars or other programs to help you apply this kind of material. However, if you are challenged by emotional intimacy you may want to consult a professional counselor for assistance. This is one aspect of marriage that especially lends itself to the individualized training an experienced therapist can provide.

Physical Intimacy

One point most behavioral science experts agree upon is that to love and be loved are basic needs of every human being. Of the many ways to communicate love for another person, expressions of physical affection are some of the most satisfying.

Our bodies and skin were meant to be touched. One frequently cited illustration that documents the universal need for "contact comfort" is the European orphans who died due to a lack of human touch. Once the caretakers started holding the babies while feeding them, deaths decreased dramatically.

Children are not the only ones who need to be touched, held, and hugged. Adults also need to be caressed, embraced, and touched in many ways. Physical intimacy between husbands and wives includes holding hands, hugging, kissing, caressing, and relating sexually with one another. Sexual intimacy is the ultimate way soulmates express their physical affection for one another.

Some argue that physical intimacy is merely "chemistry" between a male and a female. It certainly can be. That's basically what occurs when two people who have just met end up in bed together—nothing more than sexual attraction. However, thriving soulmates deserve far more than this. One of the tremendous advantages of committed life partners is that they have ongoing opportunities to express and receive physical manifestations of their mutual affection: tender moments of brushing a tear from the cheek, a neck rub to get rid of the "kinks" in life, embracing one another during times of sadness or joy, or even simply holding hands while you're walking. Naturally, marriage partners also have the benefit of expressing their love through the ultimate demonstration of physical affection: the act of sexual intercourse.

In discussing the sexual relationship between a man and woman, we want to make a very important point: Many of the practices discussed in this book can be applied not only between marriage partners, but between any individuals who want to improve their relationship. For example, we share experiences with co-workers, neighbors, and extended family. Family members and friends care for one another, confront

> 🌿 *These are the* 🌿
> *sublime moments*
> *which unite us*
> *in a special*
> *and exclusive*
> *union not shared*
> *with anyone else*
> *on earth.*

and resolve their conflicts, grow together in many ways, and develop emotionally intimate relationships. The sexual relationship, however, is different. Husbands and wives who are serious in their commitments to one another recognize a basic fact: The only person on earth with whom it is appropriate to share this ultimate expression of physical love is your marriage partner.

The sexual relationship is the only one of life's experiences which a husband and wife share uniquely with one another. In all of life's many facets, we continually share our mates with others, whether at work, with family or friends, or in the community. We share our expertise and talents as a teacher, a painter, a mechanic, a dentist—with many people around us. But in the privacy of the bedroom, we can experience oneness in our physically intimate connections. These are the sublime moments which unite us in a special, exclusive union not shared with anyone else on earth. Sexually connecting with our "soulmate" is the one practice of marriage that is uniquely powerful in its capacity to unite, bind, and renew our relationship.

> *Sexually connecting is the one practice of marriage that is uniquely powerful in its capacity to unite, bind, and renew our relationship.*

Any partner who overlooks this vital fact makes two serious mistakes. First, he or she fails to take advantage of a distinctive, delightful resource for cementing the couple's bond as exclusive and devoted lovers. Second, because sexual needs are normal and individuals naturally seek to fulfill them—in this dimension of marriage more than in any other—it is crucial that both partners do what it takes to meet one another's needs. To put it bluntly: If you don't adequately meet your partner's sexual needs, who will?

During intimate encounters, the ego boundaries between a man and woman—which normally keep us distanced from others and protect us during the course of daily life—come down. As people reach out to encompass another human being sexually, they become considerably more vulnerable. During the act of sexual intercourse, with our boundaries down, we are more likely to feel that we "love" the person we're with. Thus, sexual intimacy provides an emotional environment which can greatly reinforce the love, caring, and respect we feel for our loved one. Of course, those who have lived long enough understand that loving someone for a lifetime is very different from merely participating in a momentary, pleasurable experience.

Mutual lovemaking and the oneness created from it are the most beneficial, repeatable experiences a couple can share. In their excellent book, *The Act of Marriage*, Tim and Beverly LaHaye point out that though the amount of time a couple spends making love is quite limited (less than 1 percent), the dividends are substantial. That's because when a couple's sexual experience is pleasurable for both partners, their positive feelings toward each other during the act extend into their contentment after lovemaking.

It's virtually impossible for anyone today *not* to be exposed to an abundance of references to sex, including many fine resources covering numerous aspects of sexuality and physical intimacy. Interested couples will find no lack of information concerning differences in male and female needs, creating romance, creative ways to seduce your mate, stages and cycles of sexual arousal, techniques for lovemaking, positions during intercourse, methods of achieving orgasm—the list goes on and on.

We are fully aware of the broad spectrum of knowledge, experiences, attitudes, and values of different individuals concerning sexuality. Also, we realize that what some couples are perfectly comfortable with in the privacy of their own bedrooms might seem uncomfortable to discuss in a more public forum, or even to read about. So, even though a couple's own experiences with physical intimacy are usually "X" rated by their very nature, in this chapter we've chosen to include material of a "PG" nature. (Those wanting more explicit information about sexual relationships certainly have a wide variety of resources to draw upon.) We'll focus on twelve basic concepts about physical intimacy relevant to virtually all husbands and wives who want to share a satisfying sex life together. You'll note that the underlying assumption with all twelve is that thriving sexual relationships always require two fully participating partners.

PHYSICAL INTIMACY . . . A Lover's Dozen

1. A Wonderful Power

Sex is one of the strongest forces in the universe. The sexual urge within humans never ceases to seek fulfillment. Rather than denying or avoiding this reality, wise couples acknowledge it and find ways to channel this powerful force constructively in their marriage.

ⅅRES:

    As a professional counselor, I have occasionally met with couples who have had mixed feelings about sexuality because of a conservative "Christian philosophy." When this was the case, I encouraged them to read what many conservative Christian authors have written about physical intimacy in marriage. During the 25 years I've been in family life education, I've found that some of the more useful material developed for helping couples improve their marriages—including their sex lives—has been in selected books and tapes distributed through Christian bookstores.

    Most Christian authors who are realistic and candid—even if somewhat conservative in their views—agree on several points: (a) God created men and women as they are. This includes their sex organs, their erogenous zones, their sensual responsiveness, their sexual drives, the way their bodies respond during sexual intercourse, and so forth; (b) sex is very good and very powerful; (c) it's important for individuals to understand their sexual natures, and (d) it's desirable for husbands and wives to learn how they can make their exclusive sexual relationship become a highly effective means of reinforcing their good feelings toward each other and their mutual commitment in marriage.

Once couples realize these concepts are logical and consistent with their own value systems, they embrace the sexual dimension of their marriage relationship with openness and enthusiasm. This enables them to experience the positive power of joyful and fulfilling physical intimacy.

---

2. Between the Ears

It has been observed that the most important sexual organ of all is located between the ears. Some women worry that their breasts just aren't the right size; some men are concerned about the size of their penises; husbands and wives can both be unduly concerned if they don't have a beautiful face or a "buff body with six-pack abs" like so many of the "beautiful people" portrayed in the media.

The fact of the matter is this: A couple's enjoyment of their sexual relationship is based primarily upon two factors: (a) the attitude each partner has toward his or her own body, and (b) the identity each feels as a sexual being with a normal responsiveness to sensuality. These factors, along with a couple's open-mindedness and desire to experience joyful pleasure, are far more important to their sexual satisfaction than whether the wife happens to be gorgeous or the husband very handsome.

Remember, 99.99 percent of all men and women on earth were endowed with the basic "sexual equipment" necessary to fully enjoy sexual relations. Obviously, many married people find that doing whatever they can to enhance their physical attractiveness (through exercise, nutrition, dress, etc.) will help them feel better about themselves and will increase their mutual sexual attraction to one another as marriage partners. The point is that virtually every husband and wife—regardless of looks—has the potential to thoroughly enjoy physical intimacy in marriage.

3. Sex Education

Savvy partners make it a point to learn all they can to maximize their sexual satisfaction. This includes becoming informed about:

- The anatomy and physiology of male and female sexuality (organs, erogenous zones, and so forth).
- The phases of sexual arousal in both men and women.
- Anything else you may find interesting and useful.

4. One-on-One Private Tutoring

Perhaps the most important of all sex education occurs in one-on-one private tutoring sessions between spouses. Developing the art of mutually satisfying lovemaking is one kind of learning that is most effectively accomplished by doing. Because individual responses may vary, it's important to communicate clearly to your mate those things that feel good to you. This can be done verbally ("I like it when you . . .") and nonverbally, by guiding your partner's hand, with responsive body movements, sighs of pleasure, and so forth. Private sexual tutoring sessions with your soulmate are a very appropriate opportunity to apply the Platinum Rule.

5. Lifelong Learning

Remember, it's a mistake to assume you can predict your mate's sexual preferences based solely on previous experience. These preferences can and do change. For example, at any given time there may be a desire for "gentle, slow, and easy" or "rough and tumble horseplay," either within the same lovemaking session or from one sexual encounter to another. There might be times during a couple's sexual relationship when a wife wants to be the aggressive one and "take charge," or other times she may prefer to be "taken" by her man. Similarly, a husband sometimes wants to "lead out" in sexual encounters with his wife, and other times he enjoys the role of being the "responsive follower" to his mate's initiation of lovemaking. The key is to be always open-minded and responsive to your spouse's preferences day in and day out, year after year. Who knows what fun and creative things you might discover about your sexual partner during a lifetime of enjoyable learning?

6. Creative Exploring

Unfortunately, one perspective that some marriage partners adopt is that sexual intercourse is a conjugal duty to be endured. If either partner consistently plays a passive role, for any reason, the couple's sexual relationship will suffer greatly. They will not enjoy the benefits that a terrific physical relationship can bring to their marriage. To gain the full benefits of sex and develop a thriving marriage, both partners need to develop an adventurous spirit in the bedroom. We're not suggesting that couples need to be "far out" in their quest for "spice" in the bedroom. However, to keep the home fires burning bright, many couples find it helpful to explore new ways of expressing their love for one another. Couples don't usually determine a single best way to express their mutual affection. Rather, most partners enjoy a lifetime journey of experimenting together to discover varieties of affection. Undoubtedly, these will change over time and the different seasons of life. For this discovery to occur, both soulmates must be continually curious and open-minded about their physical intimacy, while remaining sensitive and responsive to each other's preferences.

> *Remember, find something new to do in the bedroom, not someone new to do it with.*

7. Adapting as Needed

Be sensitive to special circumstances or changing physical conditions which call for different kinds of responsiveness from your sexual partner. Three common examples are:

1. During pregnancy, certain intercourse positions are likely to be more comfortable than others.
2. If one partner has certain physical limitations or disabilities, both husband and wife can thoroughly enjoy their sexual relationship by modifying the

ways that sexual pleasure is given and received. Sexual intercourse isn't the only way to communicate physical affection.

3. As couples grow older, both partners probably need to be more patient with each other during lovemaking due to natural physiological changes, such as men's capacity to achieve and maintain an erection, women's capacity to lubricate, and so forth.

Those couples who consciously adapt both their expectations and their style of sexually relating to one another often find that they enjoy their sex lives more than ever.

8. Pleasure, Not Performance

To get the most from their sexual relationship, spouses need to concentrate on both giving and receiving pleasure. If either partner focuses attention on how well he or she is "performing," this detracts from the partners' overall sexual satisfaction. Both soulmates need to be unselfish in their efforts to please the other, but also understand themselves well enough to know how to fully enjoy their intimate moments.

Experienced couples know that not every intimate encounter needs to result in sexual intercourse to be satisfying. Sometimes partners may wish to express their physical affection without becoming sexually involved. Some wives resist intimate moments with their husbands, knowing that they always lead to intercourse. So, if they are not in the mood for full-blown, sexual intercourse, they avoid any kind of physical contact, which is unfortunate for both marriage partners.

> *Sometimes, allow your caring to be expressed in sensual ways that don't lead to intercourse.*

There are plenty of delightful ways to pleasure your partner that are sensual, but not sexual. This is one of the most important things that husbands can learn: to find enjoyment in expressing affection toward their wives in sensual, nonsexual ways. Sometimes, caring in an intimate way that doesn't lead to sex is an extremely powerful way to communicate your love for your spouse. On other occasions, couples might transform an emotionally intimate moment of sharing a feeling into a tender kiss, and then, when appropriate, into the total connectedness of intercourse.

Here's an activity designed to help husbands and wives enjoy their physical intimacy without engaging in sexual intercourse. Couples who enjoy fanciful, creative fun might want to try it out:

A SENSUOUS DELIGHT

In carrying out this exercise, remember this: Your objective is to play the role of a trustworthy friend whose sole purpose is to enhance your friend's sensuous delight. Everything you do should focus on this goal of providing a caring service to her or him, rather than on paying attention to your own personal gratification. (Individuals who are entertainers by nature might even begin by announcing to their marriage partner: "I am thy humble servant, here to attend to thine every need and provide much pleasure to every inch of thine entire body!")

In order to prepare for and fully enjoy this experience you'll probably want to turn off the television earlier than usual. Fill the bathtub with water that's a warm, comfortable temperature. Add a fragrant bath gel, oil, or bubble bath. Create soft lighting with scented candles or a dimmer switch. Have soft, romantic music (preferably instrumental) playing in the background. Invite your soulmate to step into the bathtub and prepare for a relaxing, sensuous, pleasurable feast.

Suppose the person who will enjoy this experience is your wife. Encourage her to simply recline in this luxuriant "pool of peaceful pleasure" to her heart's content, soaking up the warmth through every pore of her body. Give her a special shampoo, taking your direction from her as to what type of shampoo and rinse to use, and when to do this during her bath. It's generally most convenient for you to do this kneeling on the carpet at one end of the tub, running your fingers through her tresses and gently massaging her scalp as you cleanse her "crowning glory." When she feels totally relaxed and completely content from lingering in liquid, she's ready for the next phase.

Take her hand to assist her in stepping gingerly out of the tub. As she stands on the soft rug, dry her off, gently patting her body with a towel that you've heated up in the dryer. Ensure that in drying her off, the only thing that touches her skin is your towel, not your hands. Remember, your role in this activity is that of a "trustworthy servant," not a lover.

After you've dried her off, place a robe—also warmed in the dryer—around her. Your next task is to dry and comb her hair. Take your directions from her stated preferences in using a hair dryer, comb, or brush to dry her hair.

At this point, take her gently by the hand and lead her over to the bed, helping her take her robe off and recline in comfort on her stomach. Kneeling to one side of her on the bed, give her an almost-full body massage. Before beginning this, ensure that you have used a little lotion on your own hands to minimize any roughness. Also make sure that you have softened the ambience of the bedroom with very soft music and lighting, and that the room is reasonably warm.

Using a fragrant body lotion or oil of your choice (that you have pre-warmed slightly), gently massage her body, beginning with the tips of her toes. Massage each toe separately, doing so tenderly and deliberately. Very gradually, work your way up her ankles and calves, softly moistening the pores of her skin with every circular motion of your hands. In caressing her skin, experiment using one or several fingers simultaneously, massaging sometimes with two or three fingers, other times with the heel of your hand, and still others using your entire hand. As this particular exercise is designed to be entirely soft and gentle, all of this massaging should be gentle caressing, rather than kneading, pounding or using heavy pressure in your massaging movements.

Continue slowly up the underside of her knees and the back of her thighs, remembering to stop about three inches from her buttocks (remember, this is a sensuous—not sexual—experience). Then skip up to her waist and begin again, massaging the small of her back, all the way up her back and shoulders, then up the back of her neck, slightly massaging her scalp if she desires. If she has some real knots and kinks and would like you to do so, it's appropriate to be firmer as you massage her back and shoulders. Finally, massage the backs of her arms, her wrists, the palms of her hands, and then her fingers, one by one.

Now, encourage your wife to gently roll over and lie on her back. Once again, begin with her toes and feet and work your way up the front side of her body. This time, as you massage, stop a few inches before you get to the top of her thighs, skip her entire pelvic region and continue again at her waist, once more stopping a couple of inches below her breasts, then proceed with her shoulders and down the front side of her arms and top-side of her hands and fingers, gently working the lotion into each separate finger. Finally, ever so gently, use your fingertips to tenderly caress her chin, cheeks, nose, and forehead, once again running your fingers through her hair to massage her scalp if she so desires. In concluding this sensuous experience, gently cover your sweetheart with the top sheet and blanket, and tuck her in. You may now give her a tender kiss on the lips before turning off the music and putting out the candles.

A final reminder: Generally speaking, you should anticipate that this will be the end of the evening, with both you and your companion enjoying a full and restful sleep. We cannot guarantee, however, that occasionally you might not be awakened later from your sleep by an amorous sweetheart who now wants to engage in a continuation of your sensuous experience on a different level.

It is certainly not necessary for all couples to carry out the Sensuous Delight activity to have wonderful physical intimacy. Husbands and wives can do many different things to be sensuous without being sexual. Gently caressing a cheek or forearm, running your fingers through each other's hair, nibbling his or her ear, tenderly squeezing a knee, cuddling in bed—there's no end to the ways caring soulmates can express their affection for one another physically. As with all other aspects of their marriage, couples do best by focusing on whatever seems well-suited to their own preferences.

9. The Cause-Effect Paradox

There's an interesting paradox about the quality of a couple's sexual experience: It both reflects and contributes to their overall relationship. The sexual aspect of marriage is most affected by all other facets of the relationship. If things aren't going well in other areas of a couple's interaction, their sexual relationship tends to suffer. If partners don't share activities together, aren't kind to one another, or don't resolve problems well, they are unlikely to experience much satisfaction in bed. On the other hand, a good sexual relationship can greatly increase a spouse's positive feelings toward his or her mate and improve the couple's motivation to work on other areas of their marriage. Savvy couples recognize the "cause-and-effect" nature of sex, and use it to their mutual advantage as they seek to improve the quality of their marriage.

𝒪RES:

One of the most common problems I encounter in counseling couples is that one partner in a marriage makes the mistake of expecting that everything else in the relationship needs to be wonderful as a prerequisite for "having sex." The approach of using sex primarily as a conditional activity—either to punish or reward a mate's behavior—doesn't usually work over the long run. From a practical perspective, effective counselors usually find it more useful to help couples' sexual relationship go well as a way to increase the probability of making other, more difficult changes necessary to achieve a mutually satisfying marriage relationship.

10. Fat-Free, Fun, and Free

I once heard a seminar speaker refer to sex as a great way for couples to enjoy a shared experience that's "totally fat-free, fun, and free."

In many respects, sex is the great equalizer. Contrary to popular media portrayals, a couple need not be on an exotic vacation, drive a fancy car, or wear designer clothes in order to have a great sex life. In reality, the poorest of couples in the humblest of circumstances can have all of their sexual encounters with one another be delightful, shared experiences that renew their marriage relationship.

𝒪RES:

I've never forgotten an experience I had in counseling a couple many years ago: This couple was living on a very limited income which did not permit
them to "go out" a lot. Both husband and wife were
obese, and they lived a rather meager existence in a
lower-class part of town. During one session they said
to me: "You know, Dr. Tanner, we don't go out a lot;
we barely make enough money to make ends meet.
We don't drink [alcohol], and we're not into some of
the things other couples seem to do for fun. But boy,
do we ever have a good time in the bedroom! Sex for
us is the main thing we do for enjoyment, and it sure
makes a difference." To me, this was a perfect illustration of how any couple can enjoy the benefits of a fun
activity that is both extremely pleasurable and vitally
important to marriage, without paying anything.

---

11. Stress Reduction

To say that most people today lead stressful lives is
quite an understatement. A nice benefit of a couple's sexual relationship is that it can help both partners find some
relief from the stresses of daily living. This can occur on
both the emotional and physical levels.

Falling asleep in the arms of your sweetheart after a
long, tense day can somehow make all of your problems
seemingly melt away. Obviously, couples' challenges don't
simply go away because of a great sex life, but a satisfying
sexual experience can at least help them feel that way, if
only for a brief time. Likely, there is no other repeatable
activity in which a couple's anticipation, enjoyment, and
recollection all contribute so greatly to their need for relief
from life's "tough stuff." In some ways, then, physical intimacy in marriage functions as one of the best "perspective
restorers" ever used by men and women.

Everyone knows that orgasms automatically lead to a physical release (and hence serve as stress reducers) for men through ejaculation during intercourse. However, for women to enjoy this same stress reduction during intercourse, it is important for them to experience orgasm as well. An interesting paradox of the sexual experience is this: When a woman becomes sexually aroused but does not personally experience climax, her elevated tension level makes her feel more uncomfortable. Typically, it may take her some time before this discomfort subsides without an orgasmic release. This is an additional reason for husbands and wives to focus on making their sexual activities physically satisfying for both partners.

It's the mutual responsibility of both husbands and wives to ensure the experience is good for both. Husbands, if you will take the time to ensure your wife has a positive, fulfilling experience and also feels the sexual tension relief, it will pay off for both of you in the long run. She will enjoy the experience more, and instead of feeling frustrated or unfulfilled, she will want to experience that euphoria again and again. Satisfied wives are more likely to initiate sex with their husbands. And wives, it's your responsibility to let your husbands know what you like and what you need in physical, emotional, and mental stimulation for you to enjoy the experience.

12. Sexual Sensitivity

In spite of how wonderful sex can be for a marriage, it can also be the most problematic and sensitive facet of some couples' entire relationship. A wide variety of reasons can cause such problems.

Some individuals have a hard time feeling "sexy" because they don't like their bodies. They feel too fat or too skinny, that their shoulders are too narrow, their hips too big, their breasts too small, their face not quite the right shape—the list can go on and on. Or, perhaps there are problems in the bedroom stemming from some unresolved experience during childhood or an earlier relationship.

Our feelings about ourselves—physically and emotion-ally—influence our attitudes in the bedroom. If something is holding you back from being the sexual partner you want to be (or what your spouse needs or wants you to be) then decide what to do and make changes. For exam-ple, if you can do something about being overweight or underweight, do it. We can control many more things in our lives than most people suppose. In many instances, it's primarily an issue of wanting it badly enough.

If physical intimacy happens to be an area of concern in your marriage, take heart; there are several useful resources available. Many books and tapes do an excellent job in helping individuals and couples understand how to overcome specific problems in their sex lives. Some may find it helpful to consult with a professional counselor to deal with sensitive and problematic issues of this nature and, more importantly, to help them move forward in life. The key is to move forward. Sometimes if we look back too hard and too long, we can get "stuck" there. Too often, individuals use past experiences as an excuse for why they cannot do something. Reviewing past experiences can help us understand why we feel a certain way, but more importantly, we need to know how to move beyond the past so we can live happy, productive lives.

𝒮USAN:

I was raped when I was four years old by three teenage boys, and lived with a suppressed memory for 30 years. When the painful feelings and awful memories came flooding back, they helped me understand some of my "hangups" with sex and my inability to feel total-ly comfortable with my own body. But, after living in tears and fears for several years, I realized I had to move on in my life. It really did not matter why I had been sexually abused; it just happened. It was a terrible, exploitive, reprehensible act. That fact could never be changed. But what could be changed were my feelings of guilt, shame, anger, and resentment. I felt that I had to gain control over my feelings. This event could have permanently impacted my life in destructive ways, but I made a choice. I cannot say this was easy, but it was possible and happened for me. I never gave up on myself. I decided I was not going to let things from the past control my life and future.

This was a horrible and tragic event in my life, but I have learned that I am stronger than I ever imagined, and I can make my life whatever I want it to be. Blaming someone is wasted energy—especially blaming God. Things happen in life which we have no control over, but we do have control over our feelings. Sometimes it doesn't seem like it, but we do. I decided that I didn't want my past to dictate my future. So I "let it go." In my own case, I was greatly helped because of my faith in a Supreme Being. I know God loves me and will carry my burden when I no longer can or want to. I gave it to Him to carry; I didn't want it anymore.

———————

For anyone who has experienced traumatic events—as a child or an adult—get whatever help you need. What's important is to be encouraging, patient, and supportive with yourself or your soulmate as you deal with this highly sensitive area. This is one of life's challenges in which you need your "best friend" more than ever. This chapter explores physical and emotional connecting. Clearly, it's possible for partners to have great sex and feel intense pleasure without ever feeling love for one another. On the other hand, spouses can develop a close, loving relationship independent of physical intimacy. Ultimately, however, one of the most satisfying dimensions of a relationship is when, as a husband and wife, we experience the moments of physical pleasure, along with expanded joy within our souls, as we connect with another human being. When this occurs, we will feel we have truly connected as soulmates.

MAIN IDEAS:
Connect

- Intimacy has both an emotional and physical component.
- Emotional vulnerability is a prerequisite to emotional intimacy.
- Revealing who you really are and sharing your feelings fosters emotional intimacy.
- To love and be loved are basic needs well met by connecting with your soulmate.
- Sex has a powerful capacity to unify, bind, and renew a couple in their mutual love.
- A couple's sex life reflects and contributes to their total relationship.
- Sex is best when both partners are active participants and are responsive to each other.
- Giving and receiving pleasure—not sexual performance—is the best focus for spouses.
- The most important factor in physical intimacy is the attitude of both partners.
- Feelings about oneself influence attitudes in the bedroom.

20 QUESTIONS
to Ponder and Discuss

First, ask yourself the following questions about how you connect with your soulmate. Then discuss these questions with your soulmate by asking: "How am I doing?" and "How might we improve?"

1. Do you feel that your spouse is your true "soulmate" who you enjoy connecting with?

2. Is your marriage relationship characterized by both emotional and physical intimacy? Do you feel both heartfelt love and deep passion for one another?

3. Are you willing to risk being emotionally vulnerable in order to reap the rich rewards of an emotionally intimate marriage with your spouse?

4. Do you or your mate tend to hold back your deep inner feelings, or do you share them openly in an effort to help one another understand who you really are and who you are becoming?

5. Do either of you feel judged or criticized when expressing sensitive feelings or unsettling thoughts? How can hurtful reactions be minimized?

6. Can you or your mate identify several of each other's strongest sources of: fear, doubt, joy, pride, pain, embarrassment, hope, contentment?

7. Do you encourage each other to open up and share deep feelings about difficult, sensitive areas by being empathetic, nonjudgmental, and understanding?

8. How do you feel about yourself as a sexual being? Do you enjoy relating sexually to your partner?

9. Do you view your sexual relationship as a wonderful way to reinforce all facets of your marriage? Do you avoid using sex as a conditional punishment or reward?

10. Are you knowledgeable about male and female sexuality, the physiology of the sexual response cycle in both men and women, and other basic information on sex?
11. Are you and your mate comfortable in telling and showing each other what feels best during physical intimacy?
12. Are you both sensitive and responsive to your soulmate as a sexual partner? Do you apply the Platinum Rule in the bedroom?
13. Do you both strive to be actively engaged (rather than passively involved) in your sexual relationship? Do both partners initiate various aspects of lovemaking?
14. Is your sexual relationship characterized by creativity and adventure? Would your mate describe you as "fun-loving" during your sexual encounters?
15. Have you explored ways to adapt your patterns of physical intimacy to accommodate changing circumstances?
16. Have you cultivated ways to express your affection for one another in ways that don't involve sexual intercourse? Do these include saying "I love you" and sensuous touching?
17. Are you both enjoying the "stress reduction" benefits of intercourse by making sure that both of you experience orgasm most of the time?
18. Is there anything that has prevented either of you from fully enjoying physical intimacy in your marriage? If so, have you discussed it and taken steps to improve it?
19. Do you make every effort to sensitively support your beloved soulmate in his or her efforts to deal with any problems that may have prevented sexual enjoyment?
20. What else have you learned about the *Connect* practice (not from this book) that you can apply to your benefit?

Now What?

After evaluating where you are in the *Connect* practice, use the *KISS Marriage Maker*™ to identify goals and actions to improve those areas which need help. You might want to concentrate on one area at a time for a week or two, then move on to another area. This is an effective way to specifically improve and see the results of your efforts.

CONNECT:
Ideas to Consider

The following list of ideas might help you consider ways to connect and express your love for one another through enhanced emotional and physical intimacy.

- In a letter to your soulmate, reveal some facet of your private life that you have never before shared, with the intention of helping him or her understand you better.
- Allow yourself to cry in the presence of your spouse.
- Tell your spouse what your greatest fear is.
- Plan a night out for her ("wine and dine" her as you did when courting her).
- Plan a surprise evening for him (candlelight dinner with a sexy outfit, etc.).
- Share one of your lifelong ambitions with your spouse and discuss together if there are some specific ways he or she can support you in realizing them.
- Try this stimulating sequence:
  a. One night caress each other without touching any sexual parts or erogenous zones (no sex).
  b. The next night touch and caress each other sexually, without engaging in sexual intercourse.
  c. The next night do all of the above—but end with sexual intercourse.
- Read a book on sex together.
- Help your beloved companion gain some relief from the stresses of the day by massaging his or her back and neck. (Remember, as your soulmate's private masseur or masseuse, take your cues from your mate about specific location, firmness, softness of motions, etc.).
- Give each other a full body massage with lotion or body oil you've taken the time to warm up (tell each other what feels best).

- Describe to your sexual partner the feelings and sensations you experience when he or she caresses and touches various parts of your body in different ways.
- Try altering the physical ambience of your bedroom (scented candles, soothing music, satin sheets, and so forth).
- Take turns giving and receiving sensual and sexual pleasure (one night the wife is in control of the experience so she can receive maximum pleasure; one night the husband guides the experience to receive maximum pleasure; also alternate nights when each gives pleasure to suit your preference).
- Make love somewhere other than in the bedroom.
- Tell your companion what he or she does to satisfy you most (lovemaking positions, caresses, etc.).
- Practice verbalizing your emotional reactions, rather than your mental thoughts about various events to your mate (use words such as *hopeful, angry, delighted, insecure,* and *eager,* instead of *think, seems to me, my opinion is,* and so forth).

"It takes two to speak truth—one to speak and another to hear."

— *Henry David Thoreau* —

5

CONFRONT

*Communicate Concerns
About "Tough Stuff"
with Your Spouse*

*B*EING human means that we continually face problems in our daily lives. Thus, all husbands and wives will inevitably encounter challenges, large and small, on an ongoing basis (even those with the best marriage relationships).

It's naive to believe otherwise. This is true for all couples, regardless of how in love they are or what their financial status may be. Throughout the entire course of marriage, all couples will continue to face their own sets of challenges and must deal with their own unique blend of "tough stuff."

To effectively confront—and work through—challenges are two of the most vital skills for couples to learn. This chapter discusses why we need to confront difficult and sensitive issues and how to do this constructively as a couple. In the next chapter (*Resolve*) you'll learn guidelines for how to complete the process effectively. Confronting and resolving are two essential components of a single integrated process. We've organized the concepts into two broad categories described in Chapter 5 and Chapter 6. Thus, you should make sure you review and implement both chapters.

We must typically face a variety of issues in our individual lives, careers, children, family members and friends, and spouses. These concerns have the potential to impact our marriage relationships as well. Our personal issues frequently affect our mates, simply because we are linked in marriage.

Unfortunately, many couples are unrealistic about this fact. Whether they put their "heads in the sand" to appear "just fine," or engage in some other form of denial, they do themselves a disservice when they fail to actually confront their challenges.

The avoidance pattern is frequently set in motion by the common tendency of people, during courtship, to "put their best foot forward" and shield each other from knowing about certain difficulties or challenges they face. This can stem from a common fear that "If others only knew who I really am—or what I'm like on a bad day—they wouldn't like me." The result most feared is that this could mean the end of the relationship.

> ❧ *Whether their* ❧ *style is to put their "heads in the sand" or maintain an image of "just fine," couples do themselves a disservice when they fail to confront their challenges.*

A young couple fell into this trap during their courtship as the young man continually gave in to his sweetheart to avoid conflict because he was afraid of losing her. Consequently, they never had any arguments or disagreements before their marriage. After they were married and things had settled, he began to get tired of always giving in and started to voice his opinion on the many issues they were facing. Needless to say, this new pattern of openly expressing different views not only surprised his wife, but also brought their conflicts into the open where they could then be dealt with.

In reality, the interests of all parties are best served when they know the truth. There are definitely some important exceptions to this generalization. Wise persons use discretion and tact in "baring their souls" to one another. Wisdom and prudence suggest there are appropriate times to postpone dealing with certain problems. As a general rule, however, it's best both to acknowledge and deal with challenges rather than avoid or deny them.

Couples also fail to confront their problems because one or both spouses adopt a relationship characterized by "peace at any price." To avoid this pitfall, it's important to understand the difference between conflict and contention, as well as the difference between confronting and being confrontational.

- *Conflict* is neither good nor bad, but neutral. In marriage, it reflects the inevitable differences between any two individuals; conflicts between individuals are unavoidable and should be confronted and dealt with.

- *Contention*, on the other hand, has a very negative effect on relationships. Contention involves fighting, arguing, or bickering when there is a lack of harmony. Contentious individuals are usually quarrelsome and hostile.

- To confront is to face reality. Confronting problems effectively requires integrity, maturity, courage, responsibility, and sensitivity.

- To be confrontational is to be belligerent, abrasive, pushy, or inappropriately aggressive.

To apply the healthy practice of *Confront*, an individual must be committed to interpersonal relationships centered on truth—speaking the truth, discovering the truth, and acting upon the truth.

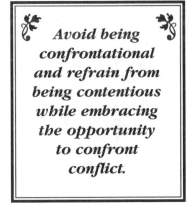

Avoid being confrontational and refrain from being contentious while embracing the opportunity to confront conflict.

So what does this mean for individuals who want both honesty and harmony in their interpersonal relationships, especially those who want a thriving marriage? Here's a piece of advice worth considering: Avoid being confrontational and refrain from being contentious while embracing the opportunity to confront conflict.

Couples pay a high price when they avoid conflict in order to avoid contention. A compulsive avoidance of conflict itself overrides the more important need to get to the root of the problem. Avoidance readily deteriorates into habits of suppressing feelings, denying reality, and shying away from the process of problem solving. Many couples tend to deny problems to minimize their impact. Also, spouses may avoid dealing with their problems because they've always had negative experiences confronting others.

When most couples think about conflict, they think of fighting (yelling, arguing, attacking, and belittling) or withdrawing (turning away, avoiding eye contact, coldness, and silent treatment). It doesn't have to be this way. Such non-productive patterns reflect either learned behavior (from observing others), or are the result of not knowing what else to do. To confront conflicts constructively, couples must view "conflict" in an entirely different way.

Rather than interpreting conflicts as evidence of something wrong with their marriage, couples can choose to view them as opportunities to grow together and make the marriage even better. Henry Kaiser said, "Problems are only opportunities in work clothes." Conflicts can be very beneficial to a marriage when confronting them leads spouses to reexamine their assumptions, beliefs, and behavior patterns, stretch their imaginations, and explore new ways to handle challenges.

The following analogy further illustrates this concept: Consider the person faced with the task of climbing a mountain. To begin in the valley floor and reach the peak of a mountain is no small task. There will be many obstacles along the path: rocks of all sizes, including gigantic boulders, crevices where one can easily get stuck, a winding trail that, in places, is extremely narrow (but always uphill), piles of loose rock where some steps inevitably cause hikers to slip backwards, sheer vertical cliffs that cannot be climbed without exceptional skill, as well as a trusted and dependable climbing partner. It takes energy, effort, endurance, patience, and skill to climb up the face of a mountain to the summit. Furthermore, it requires a willingness to expose oneself to certain risks associated with the challenges of the hike.

A climber's journey will be greatly affected by his or her attitude toward the task. If the person views the climb as a burden that's been imposed, he or she will feel resentment and anger with every step of what seems like a long and arduous trek. But, if the person sees the climb as a challenging adventure with a worthwhile goal, the experience will be very different.

How exhilarating when the goal is achieved and the summit conquered! Besides the incredible view, there is the inner satisfaction from having confronted and conquered the challenges along the way. Similarly, as you and your spouse confront and resolve conflicts together, you, too, can feel a real "high," because you will have paid the price to complete the journey. Feeling a tremendous sense of satis-

Don't stay in the valley of marital complacency— learn the "ropes" and climb to a higher level.

faction with making the difficult climb is not the only reward you'll gain. You will also find joy from the lasting benefits of a marriage relationship that's on a much higher level than it would have been had you stayed in the valley of marital complacency or given up the climb when the going got a bit tough. Your enjoyment expands as you move to a higher level of communicating.

The key is working through the conflicts successfully. You would never attempt to scale a mountain without first preparing yourself by learning how to use climbing ropes, anchor a piton, gain a handhold in difficult terrain, and so forth. Therefore, we've included a "conflict confrontation kit" to help you learn the essential skills for your trek up the mountain of marriage. It contains the basic tools to help you succeed as climbers and, hopefully, avoid some of the pitfalls along the way.

Before learning how to confront conflicts, however, everyone needs to understand one important, preventative aspect of the *Confront* practice: establishing expectations.

Establishing Expectations

We all enter marriage hoping that many of our needs and wants will be realized, and that our relationship will develop in ways that are pleasing to us. Unfortunately, these expectations often remain unspoken, and sometimes unfulfilled.

> *Being a "mind reader" was never intended to be part of a spouse's job description in a healthy marriage*

Although most marriage partners develop some awareness of each other's preferences after years of living together, this is insufficient. In a healthy marriage, being a mind reader is not part of a spouse's job description. If an individual expects something from another person, he or she must make those expectations clearly understood.

Why do couples fail to establish marriage expectations? Perhaps they:

- Have never thought about them.
- Have been disappointed in previous relationships and don't want to get hurt; so, rather than hoping for anything, they expect nothing.
- Feel so strongly about individual freedom and autonomy, they believe it morally wrong to ask anything of their mates that could be interpreted as a demand.
- Have never had any real expectations for themselves, so defining expectations for a mate is completely foreign.
- Don't believe they have any right to ask much of anything from anyone, including their spouse.
- Fear their mate's rejection.
- Don't know the "whys" and "hows" of establishing meaningful expectations.

Savvy couples recognize that failing to establish any real expectations for one another is like an employer and employee beginning a relationship with no understanding of, or agreement on, job requirements, compensation, company policies, and so forth. This marital "sin of omission" is not the kind of error two intelligent, self-respecting marriage partners would knowingly make, and yet millions make such mistakes all the time.

ℭRES:

I learned some important lessons about the *Confront* practice the hard way. I grew up in a family and culture with a strong emphasis on being positive and avoiding negativity. I avoided confronting to not be contentious or confrontational.

Throughout my previous marriage, I never made it a point to establish clear expectations with my former wife—nor did she with me. Furthermore, neither of us was very good at confronting the problems we faced. Over the course of twenty years, we were able to "get by" in our marriage by concentrating on our primary mutual interest—our children—in ways that were mostly positive. Nevertheless, we wound up paying a high price by failing to confront the difficult, sensitive issues that continued to crop up over time—as they inevitably do in any relationship.

It took me a long time to finally confront my own genuine feelings that had built up for years: I was not happy in my marriage. I felt that a part of me was dying, and I was convinced—after trying to resolve our problems with marriage counseling over a period of eight years—that the fundamental sources of unhappiness in our marriage would never change. So it was only after tremendous struggle that I made, by far, the toughest decision of my life—to terminate my marriage of over twenty years.

How much better it might have been had I been really clear—with myself and my former wife—about what I expected in marriage. Now I'm convinced that, even though it's not always easy, constructively confronting challenges with our mates is one skill every husband and wife must learn and practice.

Committed couples embrace the opportunity to establish meaningful, realistic, and mutually acceptable expectations for one another as a productive, preventative step. Four simple guidelines in establishing marital expectations are to ensure that they are: (1) meaningful, (2) realistic, (3) mutually acceptable, and (4) effectively communicated.

Meaningful Expectations

Differentiate between your needs and wants in marriage. Ask people to define their basic needs in a relationship, and most will have difficulty. *Needs* tend to be different for each of us. Two of the most common relationship needs are satisfying physical intimacy, and the sense that one's life is better with this partner than without him or her. In general, needs are those elements that must be met in order for people to feel there's a basis to begin their relationship and to maintain it. Many individuals who have terminated their relationships have expressed that the lack of having their fundamental needs satisfied led them to feel almost as though they were dying inside.

Wants represent those things we would prefer to experience with our partner, but are not absolute, mandatory requirements for beginning or maintaining our relationship. Examples of wants vary tremendously. For example, wants might include such partner preferences as: a good tennis partner, one who makes a lot of money, one who remains highly attractive (doesn't gain weight, lose hair, get wrinkles, etc.), someone who loves being around people, a romantic companion, a kind and sensitive person, or an effective, involved parent. There's really no end to what different people want in a marriage partner.

> *Establish and communicate realistic, meaningful, and mutually acceptable expectations.*

Expectations are meaningful when we have carefully considered the aspects of a relationship that are crucial to our satisfaction, as opposed to being something we would merely like. What some individuals consider a desirable want, others define as an indispensable need. Some partners would like their mate to be a good communicator (for them it is a desirable quality—a want), while others insist they will not be in any relationship unless both mates are able to express their feelings sincerely and effectively. They have determined this to be an essential characteristic—a need. Clarifying your wants and needs is very much an individual matter, but almost always requires that people know themselves fairly well.

Realistic Expectations

Here's a four-part exercise to determine how realistic your marriage expectations are:

a. Write down fifteen marital expectations.

b. Write a brief statement by each expectation, describing the effect it will have on your marriage if it is not met.

c. Ask a close friend or trusted professional for feedback about what you've written.

d. Read and discuss what you've written with your partner, asking for honest feedback about each item.

After this exercise, you may end up with only two to ten expectations considered realistic.

Mutually Acceptable Expectations

The best-sounding expectations will never be realized unless they are acceptable to both marriage partners. This exercise will help you establish expectations that are mutually acceptable. After determining which expectations your mate considers to be generally realistic, answer the following questions about each expectation separately:

a. Do I agree that this expectation is a reasonable one?

b. Is this an expectation that I am willing to support by my personal compliance?

—If so, what will I do to demonstrate my willingness?

—If not, is there anything we can discuss that would make me change my mind? Can we negotiate any conditions that would make this acceptable to me?

c. If there are no conditions to which I'd be willing to comply, can I support you in having your expectations met in a different way or by a different person? (This should not include expectations regarding sexual needs.)

Res:
One of the most interesting presentations on guidelines for a successful marriage I ever attended was entitled: "I Vow to Love, Honor, and Negotiate with You."

Effectively Communicated Expectations

The key to using the *Confront* practice in establishing marriage expectations is how you communicate them to your spouse. Most marriage partners will listen to their mates when they express serious convictions about their relationship in a sincere and forthright manner. Henry David Thoreau said, "It takes two to speak the truth—one to speak and another to hear." Although every individual needs to communicate in a way he or she feels comfortable with, you may wish to consider the following model:

Sit down facing your partner, tenderly holding both of his or her hands with your own outstretched hands. Look at your partner squarely in the eyes. Remind your companion of several reasons that you are grateful for his or her presence in your life. Then, in clear and simple terms, state the expectations you have for your marriage and for your spouse as a marriage partner. Ask if your companion has questions about any of these, and take whatever time is necessary to discuss these expectations fully. One by one, ask whether he or she is willing to support you by complying with it. This process should be repeated in turn by the other person. After your discussion, thank your spouse for his or her commitment to, and support of, the expectations with which he or she was willing to agree. Some couples benefit when they record their agreed-upon expectations to reinforce the commitment and goodwill that underscore these agreements.

Establishing meaningful, realistic, and mutually acceptable marriage expectations offers no panacea for husbands and wives. Nevertheless, when done by two mature individuals with sincerity and goodwill, this single, preventative application of the *Confront* practice can help couples avoid countless conflicts down the road, because they will have wisely invested their time to clarify some of the basic ground rules for their relationship. When couples agree to "honor and support each other," it reinforces their sense of commitment to one another. Establishing mutually agreeable expectations that can be referred back to when either spouse falls short in living up to them sets up a mechanism for joint accountability, and thus greatly reinforces their commitment. ("We agreed that neither one of us would make any purchases exceeding $150 without previous discussion, and you have violated this agreement. This is a serious matter we need to discuss and resolve.")

Just because partners may have determined some specific expectations for each other, it does not mean these will never change. As people go through different phases of their lives and marriage, they want different things from the marriage and each other. Consider how a couple's needs change from when they first get married to fifteen, thirty-five or sixty years later! Just as the individuals evolve, so does their marriage. Therefore, it's important for marriage partners to periodically review their expectations.

Now that you've learned this useful, preventative application of the *Confront* practice, here are ten applications that are especially beneficial once conflicts arise between partners:

1. Acknowledge there is a problem.
2. Deal with your emotions constructively.
3. Be sensitive to timing.
4. Request permission to discuss challenges.
5. Use tact, prudence, and wisdom.
6. Be as positive as possible.
7. Be specific in identifying the concern.
8. Use "I" messeges.
9. Attack the issue—not each other.
10. Receive the criticism constructively.

1. Acknowledge There Is a Problem

Integrity is a cardinal principle for effective living. Being honest with yourself and your mate is equally important for a healthy marriage. This requires constant evaluation of how we think and feel about the realities and interactions in our relationship.

Couples are sometimes unaware that they are avoiding their problems altogether. Consider the following signs that the problems in your marriage are being ignored:

- A continual feeling of tension between you.
- Frequent misunderstandings in your communication.
- A pattern of minor incidents escalating into full-blown crises.

It's not uncommon for marriage partners to find that once they develop the habit of openly acknowledging problems, tension begins to dissipate and they can start to resolve conflicts.

2. Deal with Your Emotions Constructively

Once marriage partners develop the habit of acknowledging problems, their tensions tend to dissipate.

Have you ever said to yourself, "If only I weren't so angry," or "If I didn't cry every time I tried to talk about it, maybe we could actually work it out"? We can deal with problems effectively when we're in control of our emotions. Angry spouses usually fail to hear what their mates have to say, much less respond to them in a reasonable way.

We often confuse two things: the behavior of another and our own emotional reactions. This is why we're likely to say, "He makes me so mad!" or "She drives me crazy!" These are excuses; no one else can "make" us feel anything. Our mates' actions can affect us, but we ultimately choose (consciously or subconsciously) how we're going to feel about their behavior. Whenever we get upset with our spouses, we're letting their problems become our problems.

When you get upset, ask yourself: "Do I react, or am I in control of my response?" It's important to understand as much about ourselves as possible, although this sometimes means facing unpleasant realities about ourselves.

> *It's normal to have angry, resentful, or hurt feelings toward our mate. However, when we allow such emotions to persist, or we choose to dwell on them, they inevitably will be destructive to our marriage.*

Most of us have full-blown emotional reactions when we get extremely angry and feel it's "the last straw." When our outburst is over, how do we feel? Do we justify our behavior by rationalizing, "They made me so mad, I couldn't control myself"? This is a behavior pattern we develop over time. It doesn't mean it's right or even works for you; it's just a habit. Ask yourself: "As a couple, are we able to resolve the issues, or do our emotional reactions and behavior only make the situation worse?" If changes need to occur for you to respond in a controlled way, then take this opportuntiy to learn how.

Here are a few ways that can help:

A. Recognize Your Emotions

We must acknowledge our emotions for what they are and how they affect us. Because of feelings, we experience not only the "down side" of life, but also the positive emotions of joy and happiness. Ironically, we cannot know joy unless we've felt sorrow. Many individuals are convinced that the magnitude of their joy is directly correlated with the intensity of sadness they've felt. Therefore, it's important to give ourselves permission to feel our full range of emotions.

*S*USAN:

"Stuffing" my emotions was a significant problem I had in my previous life. (I call it my previous life, because I've done so much since then to change the way I view and react to the world and face life.) I am a peacemaker. I would do anything to keep peace in the home and in the family, and this became a significant problem for me in my previous marriage. I was a classic avoider. I believed that conflict was a clear sign that something was "wrong" in our relationship. I felt if I ignored the things that bothered me, they would go away and it would get better. Rarely did we bring up problems we needed to discuss, so we never became very good at solving them. So I began to stuff and stuff and stuff. Eventually, there was no room left to stuff the emotions that had built up over eighteen years, and I was in trouble.

It took years for me to deal with these "stuffed emotions" and the results of avoiding issues. I learned the hard way to deal with things as they come up, and that putting them off only leads to more problems. It is still a challenge for me not to fall into old patterns, and I still have to force myself to confront the issues as they arise.

Those who deny or "stuff" their feelings inevitably realize there's no more room to stuff, and all the emotions they've denied over the years come back to overwhelm them. Emotions have to be recognized and dealt with—now or in the future. So, take the opportunity to feel whatever emotions your life brings you; deal with them appropriately, and try not to react to them.

> *Acknowledge, verbalize, and feel your negative emotions—just don't act on them.*

All marriage partners will occasionally feel resentment, frustration, and anger toward their mates. Though it's normal to have negative feelings toward our spouses, when we allow such emotions to persist and fester, they will be counterproductive to our marriage, making it impossible to constructively resolve marital conflicts. Everyone needs to learn how to work through negative feelings quickly. (*Feeling Good: The New Mood Therapy*, by David Burns, M.D., gives useful information regarding this topic.)

When dealing with problems, if you're feeling out of control, take the time you need to process your feelings and get them under control. Go for a walk, work out, slowly sip a tall glass of lemonade or a mug of herbal tea, hoe weeds, shovel snow—whatever it takes to move yourself out of the situation and determine how to respond appropriately. If either of you is feeling stressed, give a "cue" and then withdraw to regain control. Rather than running away from problems, this is actually a practical strategy to "re-group" until emotional control is restored and an objective perspective established.

Choosing how we feel about our experiences also helps us deal with them—especially past experiences that can haunt us. If there's a past trauma that has not been dealt with, feelings from the trauma return, influence your life, and a choice must be made. Accept the feelings generated by the experience. Don't judge the feelings as "good" or "bad," but merely as emotions that exist. Then, ask yourself: What good are they doing me? Are they affecting me in a negative way? What do I need to let them go? Would it help to confront my mate and tell him or her how I feel?

Regardless of how bad an event may have been, neither you nor your mate can change the past. Therefore, it's best to minimize references to most negative past events and focus on present behaviors that need to be resolved. Focus on what you can do now to work toward a more satisfactory future together.

Minimize references to past resentments and concentrate on present constructive energies for a better future together.

B. Reframe the Situation

No matter how strong our feelings, we can use our

thoughts to channel them constructively. We need to accept problems for what they are right now in our life. Once we've accepted a problem for what it is (and is not) we can begin to "eat the elephant, one bite at a time."

> *We don't have to **like** our problems, but we do need to **accept** them for what they are, and for what they are not.*

Many of us react to our problems with "It's the end of the world," "That can never be fixed," or "She's going to kill me!" In reality, however, the problem is not going to mean the end of the world, and it probably can be resolved. We can "reframe" problematic situations by changing the way we view them. Avoid statements of helplessness or hopelessness ("We'll never be able to do it," "She won't listen," or "I'll never get through this.") Such thoughts reinforce a negative view of the world. Instead, create a positive perspective of the world and its problems: "It's hard, but we'll both be stronger when we get through it," "She doesn't seem to listen, but I will look for opportunities to discuss it with her," or "We don't quite know how we can solve this, but we'll find a way, somehow!" Change your attitude, and the world might change, too!

Face problems in a positive way, rather than "charging ahead," armed and ready for war. You can choose how you will feel about whatever comes your way. Viewing conflicts and problems as opportunities for growth is a step in the right direction; it opens the door so you can go through it together to make things better for both of you.

C. Ask "What Can I Learn?"

Life is the ultimate classroom, and every experience we have can and should be a teacher. Ask yourself: "What can I learn from this?" It may be a really big "a-ha" that changes you forever. Perhaps it makes you determined to prevent it from happening again, or you come to the conclusion "I'll never do that again!" Remember the *Transformers* toys?

It was amazing how an ordinary dump truck could be transformed into "a mighty fighting machine to destroy evil aliens from outer space." That's how you need to approach problems in your marriage. Transform your daily challenges into learning opportunities.

Children have a natural fascination with life; everything they do is a learning experience. Have you ever watched children learn to turn over, crawl, or walk? Every move they make—even falling—gives them the experience they need to do it better. Oh that we could reclaim that childlike attitude and realize that our mistakes can be our greatest teachers! If we always have to be "right" about everything, or do everything the "right" way, little room is left for us to make mistakes in life and thus learn from them.

*S*USAN:

This is one concept I've had to learn the hard way. In the past, I was fearful of making mistakes. My view of the world was that if I said the wrong thing, did the wrong thing, or made a bad decision, this somehow meant that I was a bad person. Therefore, I lived my life in fear of the consequences of my mistakes.

We can become paralyzed by our fear of making mistakes or of being perceived as "bad" because we did something wrong. We need to remember to separate the action from the person. As parents, we still love our children when they do something wrong, and we try to teach them that what they did was wrong—not that they are "bad." As marriage partners, we need to treat our mates in the same way. Actions or attitudes can be bad, but people themselves are inherently good.

I struggle every day to remember this principle as I face my challenges of life and continue to change my view of the world.

3. Be Sensitive to Timing

When confronting challenges with our mates, timing can be everything. Typically, we react to our mates at the worst possible times—usually at the height of our intense emotional response to a problem. We tend to blurt out our feelings the moment they surface within us. But this is usually the worst time to confront—much less attempt to deal with—the problem. Sometimes we need a cooling-off period. Once we've sorted through our feelings and regained emotional control, we're in a much better position to work through the problem.

> *The height of intense emotional feelings can be the worst time to confront—much less attempt to deal with—conflict.*

Make sure the time you select is good for both of you. Poor timing to raise an issue would be when your spouse walks in the door from work and hasn't even sat down yet, is engrossed in a game, TV show, or big project, or is stressed out for any reason. If your spouse is a "night owl" and you are a "morning lark," don't try to wake your spouse at 6:00 a.m. to discuss a concern; it will probably only backfire! If your life is fast-paced, try to find times when both of you are relatively non-stressed to address your problems.

4. Request Permission to Discuss Challenges

Sometimes you know the timing is bad; other times you need to ask your spouse if it's a good time to confront a challenge by requesting permission to discuss it. Working through issues is totally different when your spouse is ready to listen. Consider your reaction to the following scenarios:

a. "I'm really upset about . . ."
   "You told me you were going to . . ."
   "I can't believe you did that!"

versus

b. "I need to discuss something I'm feeling frustrated about. Is now a good time for us to talk?"

Your companion will more likely engage with you constructively if he or she feels that you have shown respect by asking if this is a good time to discuss a challenge. Such a response will also let you know if your spouse is feeling receptive to dealing with whatever is coming. As a rule, if a partner's response is, "No, now is not a good time," then he or she should specify another time that would be better. Both mates need to confirm another specific, agreed-upon time and be sure to follow through with the discussion.

If it's not a good time for you, you need to communicate this constructively by saying something like, "I'm not sure I can handle one more thing today; can we wait until [later tonight, tomorrow, a specific future time] so I can deal with it better?"

Giving a brief explanation of why you would prefer to wait also helps—so it doesn't appear you're avoiding: "It's been a really hard day at work—can I have a few minutes to unwind and regroup?"

5. Use Tact, Prudence, and Wisdom

To confront issues tactfully, think about your companion's feelings in determining how to approach the issue. Consider how you would like to be approached if the situation were reversed. Choose your words carefully; sensitivity is always appropriate.

A practice widely advocated by mental health professionals during the 1970s was to "be completely honest and candid" in sharing feelings with other people. Unfortunately, numerous couples destroyed their marriages when following this advice fully. Although honesty is important in a healthy marriage, there are times when it's best to be tactful, in addition to being truthful.

Once you've decided an issue needs to be discussed, it's not always beneficial to express the full scope of your negative feelings. Be prudent and exercise good judgment in determining how much should be said about sensitive issues. Important questions to answer are:

- "Will it benefit our marriage if I am 100 percent open in communicating my feelings about this issue to my spouse?"
- "Can I express my concern about it without going into a lengthy discourse?"

Remember, this is your best friend, and you don't want to hurt your friend or lose his or her friendship.

6. Be as Positive as Possible

Give positive feedback before launching into negative aspects of an issue you want to confront. Beginning your discussion by emphasizing positive points is sometimes helpful. For example, "Sweetheart, I have noticed how kind and sensitive you are when you talk to our neighbors; you have such compassion for others. But when you talk to me, I rarely feel a sense of kindness. It would mean a lot to me if you spoke to me with compassion, also."

7. Be Specific in Identifying the Concern

Some discussions are ineffective because of the way topics are brought up. For example, if you refer to the problem in a generalized way ("We're still having money problems; how are we ever going to pay all of the bills?") it can send up a red flag and create a "Here we go again" or "turn-off" reaction from your spouse. This is especially true if it is an ongoing issue brought up week after week. Continual reminders about problems are tough enough to handle, but when these are expressed as negative generalizations, they can be interpreted as "nagging."

More effective is identifying the specific issue you'd like to resolve and labeling it a "concern" rather than a "big problem." For example: "I'm concerned about the amount of interest we're spending on credit cards, and would like to discuss our options for paying off our credit cards so we can get out of debt." Communication experts have long known this simple truth: "A problem well-stated is a problem half-solved."

8. Use "I" Statements

One of the best techniques to confront conflicts is the use of "I" statements. This is a constructive way to assertively deal with difficult situations. There are two simple steps in formulating "I" statements:

- Describe the behavior or situation that's a problem for you:

    "When the kitchen is left a mess . . ."
    "When the phone rings and rings . . ."
    "When clothes are left all over the floor . . ."
    "When I hear a raised voice . . ."

- Describe your response to this behavior or situation. Your response might be an emotion:

    "I feel hurt, angry, helpless, guilty . . ."

    Or an action:

    "I yell, withdraw, want to walk out of the room . . ."

Examples of "I" statements are: "When clothes are left all over the floor, I get angry and feel like walking out of the house" or "Whenever I try to hug or kiss you, it seems that you pull away. I feel rejected and cut off in my efforts to connect."

"I" statements can be used when you're not quite sure what to say, but need to open the discussion. They're intended not as a means of resolving issues, but as a way to begin the process of constructively working through your challenges as a couple. The most effective "I" statements are expressed not to force mates to change, but rather to let them know how you feel about your interactions. Sometimes the most important person you're making the "I" statement for is yourself. It can clarify in your own mind what is happening and how you feel about it. Saying, "You did this" or "You did that" is almost always a way to trigger

> *"I" statements can be used when you're not quite sure what to say, but need to open the discussion.*

a defensive reaction and start a fight. Try to avoid using the word "you," but describe the behavior or action instead.

When using this method to share a personal viewpoint with your mate, give a concise summary of your reaction to a problem. Using "I" statements might be viewed as a simple way to give your husband or wife a "wake-up call." In some instances, this may be all that's necessary to prompt your mate to change his or her behavior in a way that solves the problem and, therefore, eliminates your negative response.

This should not, however, be your expectation. Communicating in this fashion merely signals your displeasure about something in a non-threatening way. Thus, it's less likely to provoke the defensive reaction common when an individual receives negative feedback. How your husband or wife chooses to respond to your "I" messages is up to him or her. The reaction will also be influenced by a variety of other factors.

9. Attack the Issue—Not Each Other

It's normal to have intense feelings about problems in your marriage. However, these feelings need to be directed toward the issue—not each other.

Res:

Some twenty years ago, as a Family Relations Professor, I used a ten-minute training film entitled "Handling Marital Conflict." The film depicts two couples, each in the middle of an argument dealing with the very same issue as it affects their marriage. The film illustrates several key principles for effective conflict resolution.

The husband and wife who are intense in expressing their upset feelings toward one another—even to the point of yelling at each other—are able to resolve their conflict because they apply so many correct principles of conflict resolution, including apologizing to each other for losing their tempers and for calling each other "stupid." The other couple is much more controlled in their expressions of negativity, with no shouting whatsoever, but rather communicates a cold, sarcastic disrespect for each other. This couple fails miserably in working through their issues for the opposite reason the first couple succeeds. Once the latter couple resorts to treating each other with meanness and disrespect, every other aspect of their discussion only serves to reinforce their bitterness toward one another.

In confronting problems and dealing with "tough stuff," couples do best when they can control their anger and frustration and deal with each other in a relatively calm manner. Perfect self-control, however, is not always necessary. It is essential, however, that both marriage partners maintain at least a minimal level of respect for each other and treat one another with some degree of dignity. It's nearly impossible for spouses to feel respected if their mates resort to name-calling, sarcastic remarks, or other "below the belt" tactics.

A destructive habit common with couples is playing the "who's right and who's wrong" game. Make sure your discussions focus on solving the problem, rather than on who's to blame.

10. Receive Criticism Constructively

We've discussed ways to confront issues when you bring them up. Equally important, however, is learning how to receive a confrontational message communicated by your mate. Even when your companion follows all the right principles in communicating criticism constructively, it can still be tough to sit, listen, and learn from criticism that's aimed directly at us. C. Darrell Langley offers guidelines for receiving criticism in his article "Constructive Criticism," found in the December 1996 edition of *Personal Excellence*:

- Take it gracefully. Take a comment at face value, avoid reading more into it than what was said, and remember, the intent is to foster improvement.
- Be objective. Don't take it personally. Focus on the subject as emotionally detached as possible, without appearing disinterested.

- Respond tactfully. Ask clarifying questions. Ask for specific suggestions for improvement.
- Make use of criticism. Correct at least one mistake or weakness as soon as possible.

RES:

    An early personal encounter with this principle occurred during my first year in graduate school. After conducting a "live" counseling interview with a couple in front of the class, our instructor, Dr. Sam McDill, began the class discussion by asking if anyone had noticed anything he might have overlooked during the session. He stated, "I'd be quite interested if any of you could recommend anything I might have done to improve my intervention during the counseling session." This was a superb way to model how a mature person can prevent becoming defensive by taking the initiative to ask others for constructive criticism. Husbands and wives could benefit greatly by applying this practice when they feel up to learning from each other's feedback, rather than reacting to it.

Most of us may need to work on receiving criticism constructively. As with anything else, practice makes perfect. Continue to practice in any areas that are a challenge, and you'll find yourself making progress.

> **Focus on "how can we solve the problem" rather than "who's to blame."**

As we indicated at the beginning of this chapter, to effectively resolve conflicts in marriage, spouses must know how to initially confront their problems well. As couples implement the skills outlined in this chapter, their ability to deal with their differences and resolve their problems will be greatly enhanced.

Confronting our challenges effectively, with sensitivity and respect, reinforces a sense of tranquility and comfort during otherwise stressful times. Knowing that we don't have to attack one another to address differences helps us maintain a pleasant relationship with each other. Applying the *Confront* practice in these ways contributes to our over-all feelings of happiness and joy—in life and with one another.

MAIN IDEAS:
Confront

- Marriage partners must continually face "tough stuff."
- Confronting difficult issues is the necessary first step to resolving them.
- Conflicts are not necessarily negative, but can offer growth opportunities for couples.
- Spouses should avoid contention but confront conflict.
- Confronting difficult issues requires integrity, maturity, responsibility, openness, and sensitivity on the part of both spouses.
- Establishing realistic, mutually acceptable expectations is an effective, preventative application of the *Confront* practice.

10 Guidelines to Confront Conflict as a Couple:

1. Acknowledge there is a problem.
2. Deal with your emotions constructively.
3. Be sensitive to timing.
4. Request permission to discuss challenges.
5. Use tact, prudence and wisdom.
6. Be as positive as possible.
7. Be specific in identifying the concern.
8. Use "I" messages.
9. Attack the issue, not each other.
10. Be receptive to criticism.

20 QUESTIONS
to Ponder and Discuss

First, ask yourself the following questions about how you and your spouse confront challenges. Then discuss these questions with your spouse by asking: "How am I doing?" and "How might we improve?"

1. How do I view the problems, conflicts, and "tough stuff" that occur in our personal lives and in our marriage?
2. Do I relate to our problems as challenges that give us opportunities to learn and become better?
3. Do I perceive our conflicts as signs of our inevitable differences, and focus on dealing with these differences?
4. Do I tend to deny problems or avoid confronting the challenges in our relationship? If so, why?
5. Have I avoided conflict to avoid contention? Have I avoided confronting problems to avoid being confrontational?
6. Are my moods governed by other people or circumstances, or do I assume personal responsibility for my feelings and how I respond to problems?
7. Have I clearly determined and defined expectations for my marriage partner? Have we openly discussed these and mutually agreed upon them?
8. Do I try to quickly work through destructive feelings rather than dwell on them?
9. If either of us is out of control emotionally, do we withdraw and "regroup" so we can work through the conflict calmly?
10. Do I "reframe" problematic situations to view and deal with them more positively?
11. Do I help clarify the real issues early in the process of confronting conflicts?
12. Do I consider timing issues in our efforts to confront difficult, sensitive issues?

13. Am I conscious of my spouse's mood, energy level, or other involvements when I bring up problems to discuss?

14. In initiating discussions about conflict areas, do I show respect by requesting permission to confront them?

15. Am I receptive when my spouse brings up difficult, sensitive issues for discussion?

16. If I don't accept my spouse's invitation to confront an issue, do I suggest a specific time when I will be willing to engage in a discussion?

17. Do I identify my concerns as specifically and constructively as possible?

18. Do I use "I" messages as a non-threatening way to share my perspective and give feedback?

19. If I have intense feelings about different issues, do I attack my spouse or the problem?

20. What else have I learned about the *Confront* practice (not from this book) that I can apply to our benefit?

Now What?

After evaluating where you are in the *Confront* practice, use the *KISS Marriage Maker*™ to identify goals and actions to improve those areas which need help. You might want to concentrate on one area at a time for a week or two, then move on to another area. This is an effective way to specifically improve and see the results of your efforts.

CONFRONT:
Ideas to Consider

The following are specific things you can do in the process of confronting challenges in your marriage:

- Make a list of ten problems that have led to conflict in your marriage. With each of these:
    —Identify whose problem it is (mine, my spouse's, ours).
    —Determine its long-range impact (will it matter one week, one year, or ten years from now?).
    —Evaluate its importance (small, moderate, large).
- When you get angry, step back and take a minute to examine why. Make a mental note or write the reason down to help you understand yourself better and why you do the things you do.
- Remind your spouse of three specific ways your marriage will benefit as each of you consistently confronts your challenges.
- When you encounter a problem, say to yourself, "I will choose how I feel about this and how I'll deal with my emotions."
- Reframe your conflict resolution discussions by beginning your conversations with phrases like:
    "Here's another opportunity for us to learn more about each other . . ."
    "Just think how we'll feel after we've taken our marriage to the next level . . ."
    "I wonder how our relationship will improve this time, after we've handled this conflict well . . ."
    "One more chance for us to stretch and grow . . ."
- Remind your mate of three ways your relationship will improve as you learn to constructively confront your challenges together.

- View your problems constructively by using words like "challenge," "stretch," "test," "growth experience," or "learning opportunities."
- Set up a regular weekly time to discuss your challenges. Schedule these in your planner and follow through without fail for at least three weeks.
- Prior to confronting a conflict with your mate, remember these two ideas: "How can I confront without being confrontational?" "How can I focus on the conflict and not be contentious?"
- Carry out the exercise on page 117 to establish realistic marital expectations.
- Help each other use better timing in confronting conflicts by making a list of good and bad times to deal with problematic, sensitive issues.
- Identify at least one point of agreement you can share with your mate prior to giving any negative feedback.
- When on the receiving end of your mate's criticism, say the following: "I value your feedback, so please help me know some additional ways I can improve in this area."
- Practice repeating to yourself when you get angry: "I have chosen to be angry, and I can change this choice by reframing the situation or asking myself, 'What can I learn from this?' "
- Follow this three-part exercise to change old habits and behaviors:
    a. Identify one behavior or habit in dealing with conflict that you would like to change.
    b. Decide what new habit you'd like to develop to replace the one you're changing.
    c. List five things you're going to do to begin using the new habit you've selected.
- When you're upset over something, ask yourself: "Whose problem is it?" This will take reflection and evaluation; if it is your problem, do something about it!

- If you find yourself attacking your mate, remind yourself: "It's the two of us against this problem. Let's focus our energy to attack this challenge, not each other!"

"In the middle of difficulty lies opportunity."

— *Albert Einstein* —

RESOLVE

*Deal with Differences and
Resolve Conflicts
with Your Helpmate*

&N THIS chapter we'll discuss additional principles you can apply to complete the process of resolving conflicts in your marriage. A willingness of both partners to do what is necessary to work through their problems is the key to solving those problems.

Two fundamental skill sets for effective conflict resolution are:

   **1. Learning to understand and deal
    with differences, and**

**2. Gaining competence in the process
of conflict resolution.**

Deal with Differences

Marriage partners can expect some conflict because of inevitable differences between two people in any relationship. Such differences include the families each spouse grew up in, their previous experiences as individuals, personality and temperament variations, and gender differences due to biological makeup and learned cultural roles.

The fundamental reality is that differences between you and your mate have always existed and will always remain.

Many husbands and wives seem to have a hard time accepting this fact. They feel attacked, misunderstood, or take it personally whenever it's clear their mate is different in any way.

It saves a great deal of unhappiness when spouses accept this fact and learn how to deal with their differences, rather than fight them. (In *Men Are from Mars, Women Are from Venus,* John Gray offers many ways for husbands and wives to both understand and deal with these differences.)

*R*ES:

One fundamental difference between Susan and me affects our interaction and used to trigger a lot of tension when we communicated, until we became aware of this difference through a seminar Susan attended.

I am an external processor and problem solver, while Susan is an internal processor and problem solver. I work through issues and problems by talking them out. My style is to analyze, explore the pros and cons of alternative solutions, and then determine which option seems best through joint discussion. Susan, on the other hand, prefers to analyze and review possible solutions in her mind before she's inclined to discuss them. She needs to sort through her feelings, determine the issues, and evaluate what the possible solutions are and what their implications mean to her before she comes to a preferred solution, and before she wants to talk. (She feels she can go through this process a lot faster in her mind than in verbal discussion.)

This is a fairly significant difference between two people (and we've found it to be a common one) that can lead to tremendous frustration as any two people attempt to communicate their feelings and solve problems.

One day in the car I brought up a problem we needed to solve and began talking about it and what I thought it meant, along with some possible alternatives. Susan was staring out the window when I asked her, "Are you mad or upset about this? Don't you want to talk about it?"

She looked at me, and then it hit me: "You're processing, aren't you?" I said. She said, "Yes. I'm not mad—just thinking it through."

It's important that I understand she's not mad, just thinking. It helps when she verbalizes this—"let me think about it"—before going inside her head. We're still working on how to merge our styles so we can communicate and solve without driving each other crazy.

Whether the differences between you are due to gender or simply to the fact that you are two unique persons, learn how these variations can benefit your marriage. The very differences between you can complement each of your individual lives in areas where either one may be deficient. Besides, wouldn't it be boring to be married to a "clone" of yourself? Marriage—like the rest of life—is interesting because of the diversity of the partners.

*S*USAN:

One of the many differences between Tres and me is our basic orientation to life. I'm very "grounded" and practical in my general approach to daily living. I focus on "current realities" and am preoccupied with making sure the bills are paid on time and that we have stability and consistency in our temporal life (things like health and life insurance, a retirement plan, and so on). Tres, on the other hand, in his effort to make a positive difference in the lives of people, is always looking two decades down the road, trying to "change the world." His dreams, scope, and vision are unparalleled by anyone I've ever met, although he sometimes "blows me away" with the magnitude of his goals.

We've learned that we need both of our styles. With me paying attention to our current needs and realities, we can move forward toward many of Tres's goals and dreams that we now share (even though they're much larger than I ever would have imagined!).

So, rather than spend endless hours arguing about whose approach is "right" or "wrong," we've learned that it's far more productive to view these differences as strengths that benefit one another. Tres has learned to appreciate and depend upon my "groundedness" to balance his life. On the other hand, I've enjoyed expanding my vision to include many of his dreams, with the depth and breadth they add to my life.

As two individuals attempting to deal with the differences between you, it's best if both of you:

- Acknowledge that many differences are inevitable.
- Accept your mate in spite of how he or she is different from you.
- Focus on ways the differences can help you as individuals and as a couple.
- Try to minimize differences by understanding and modifying your own style (like internal/external processing in our example).

Resolve Conflicts

As you attempt to resolve conflicts together, it helps to know what to do and what not to do. Here are some useful principles and practices conducive to conflict resolution:

1. *Promptly and regularly resolve conflicts.*
2. *Listen and learn.*
3. *Be patient, tolerant, and empathetic.*
4. *Clarify what the "real" issues are.*
5. *Work on one conflict at a time.*
6. *Build upon points of agreement.*
7. *Stay solution-focused.*
8. *Ask for changes that will make things better.*
9. *Apologize and forgive.*
10. *Seek mutually acceptable solutions.*

1. Promptly and Regularly Resolve Conflicts

Have you ever noticed that you're likely to "brush off" minor problems because they're not worth the irritation? Then, some conflicts are so big, they almost send you over the edge? These are likely to be ignored, mostly because we don't want to deal with something so tough. (Hopefully, these are few and far between!) In turn, many of our conflicts are of the moderate variety. They may create some frustration or tension, but aren't monumental, so they, too, are let go.

Unresolved issues build upon one another until a small problem becomes a moderate—and then big—problem. Whether large, medium, or small, unresolved conflicts emerge again. They may be with a different person or situation, but they will be the same conflicts.

Gunny Sacks and Camels' Backs

"Gunny-sacking" occurs when couples sweep conflicts under the carpet as an avoidance mechanism, hoping the problems will somehow disappear. Instead, the conflicts accumulate until there's a lot of debris under the carpet— dirty straw, mostly. A husband and wife might be discussing a minor issue (you know, one of those really big problems like who forgot to turn off the hall light), and once they start arguing, they bring up other stuff—essentially, unresolved issues. Why is this? All of the old, accumulated debris they were sweeping under the carpet was actually stuffed into their gunny sacks, and once the two of them finally "get into it," out come both gunny sacks filled with their backlog of unresolved conflicts—which naturally get dumped into the pile again.

Remember the adage "the straw that broke the camel's back"? Well, in relationships, the gunny sacks filled with the straw of unresolved issues are heaped on camels. These camels—the mute martyrs in marriage—simply continue to accept an ever-increasing load from their cop-out couple masters. Finally, however, the load is just too much to bear—even for these uncomplaining beasts of burden. The husband or wife tries to stuff a final straw into the bulging gunny sack on the camel, and the poor beast just keels over onto the desert sand—its back broken by one too many straws of unconfronted, unresolved issues.

So how can couples prevent overflowing burlap bags and injured camels? By dealing with problems as they occur, on a regular, routine basis. But what does that mean? Some have suggested this be done on a daily basis, like before going to bed each night. For most of us leading busy, over-programmed lives, finding the time to deal with such conflicts every day is unrealistic. On the other hand, doing this once a month is probably too infrequent for most couples.

Our recommendation is this: Set aside a regular time each week to discuss challenge areas in your marriage. Thus, regardless of which spouse wants to deal with a problem, both know they'll have a predetermined block of time to deal with and resolve their negative feelings about each other. Naturally, some issues demand your immediate attention, but most can be dealt with during a weekly "resolve session."

> *By having a scheduled time each week to air feelings and work through conflicts, marriage partners can focus more of the limited time they have together on positive interactions.*

Having a regular time to "empty the gunny sacks" has another important advantage. If both partners know there will be a specific time each week to air their feelings and work through their conflicts, it can help them focus more of their limited time together on positive interaction. After all, wouldn't you rather spend your precious time together on an enjoyable, pleasant level?

Although it helps to deal with our marital conflicts right away, it's important to recognize that we may not always be able to resolve them immediately. Depending on the nature and complexity of the problem, it may take more time to determine the best possible solution. Couples who attempt to resolve some conflicts can quickly limit their options of possible solutions.

Also, the amount of time and energy required (up front and along the way) will vary according to the risk of the conflict. If there's a lot of personal risk involved for either partner, it will take longer to determine causes, feelings, reactions, and possible solutions. Also, it may take longer for one spouse to work through his or her feelings about it (what it means and what it will take to solve it) to take steps to correct it. So, why bring up an issue if we cannot solve it immediately? It's necessary to acknowledge that it exists in order to begin any productive discussion about it (remember the *Confront* practice). It's okay to slow down when you're evaluating why a conflict exists and what can be done about it.

If you decide to let a seemingly small problem go because it's not worth dealing with (you determine: "This won't matter six months or ten years from now"), then make sure you let it go completely. Don't let it sit and "eat at you" subconsciously, or it will turn into a big issue down the road.

2. Listen and Learn

If either spouse is totally focused on arguing his or her own point of view and proving his or her ideas are superior, the person never really understands the partner's perspective. The couple is engaged in a monologue, rather than a dialogue or discussion of ideas. To overcome this problem, implement the fundamentals of effective communication and express your opinions tentatively.

> *By using "active listening," even if you don't agree with each other, at least you can both understand one another.*

Communication is a two-way process, and occurs only when a person receives a message as it was intended by the sender. The sender sends the message, and the receiver interprets the message. It is the responsibility of both parties to ensure messages are sent and received appropriately. The active listening technique is a very useful method, especially when there is disagreement or differing points of view about an issue.

As the sender of a message:

I need to state my point of view clearly and precisely, and watch for signs indicating whether my spouse has understood or misunderstood my message. The message includes not only the words that are said, but the tone of voice and any associated body language. A key role I play in communicating messages is to ensure my mate has accurately heard and understood what I have conveyed.

Here's a very simple illustration of how this concept might be applied: "I'd like to make sure you know how I feel about this matter." After expressing your view, you might follow it up with: "Can you summarize your understanding of what I just said, so I'll know if I expressed myself clearly and you heard me correctly?"

As the receiver of a message:

I need to restate the message sent by my spouse until he or she agrees that I have accurately heard the message that was sent. Only then should I attempt to communicate my personal response. By using this "active listening" technique, both parties ensure that they correctly hear the other's point of view. This process ensures that, even when marriage partners may not agree with each other, they at least understand one another.

Numerous books and tapes have been developed over the years to help couples learn useful techniques for effective communication. If communication is a challenge in your marriage, you may want to review some of these resources for assistance. Remember, even if you do not arrive at a mutually agreeable solution, if you have heard and understood your partner's point of view, you will feel better about engaging in the conflict resolution process together, and will feel better about each other.

A simple way to listen to each other (and thus, learn from one another) is to express your personal views about an issue in tentative terms. Spouses are always on shaky ground when acting as though their own perspectives are absolutely true and correct. A far more reasonable and effective approach is to offer your viewpoint as just that—your personal perspective that you acknowledge may not be entirely accurate.

Consider how the following phrases invite further dialogue and reinforce listening and learning on the part of both partners:

- "It seems to me . . ."
- "Could it be . . ."
- "I'm not really sure, but maybe . . ."
- "My opinion is . . . What's your view . . . ?"
- "Perhaps . . ."
- "The way I see it is . . . How do you see it . . . ?"

3. Be Patient, Tolerant, and Empathic

Patience and tolerance are in the job description of every healthy marriage. This is certainly true as partners seek to resolve their problems. Some dilemmas are not resolved quickly or easily. On other occasions, circumstances, complexities or time constraints mean that a couple cannot come up with solutions efficiently. In the fantasy world of television, we see problems worked through in thirty to sixty minutes. This sometimes makes it hard for couples to be patient with themselves, each other, and the process of problem-solving in the reality of their own marriages. Nevertheless, developing patience is not only helpful, but absolutely necessary. Plautus put it this way: "Patience is the best remedy for every trouble." Tolerance, too, is crucial. To do tough things under pressure, stress, or discouragement, we can all use the support of a tolerant helpmate. What's more, we need to be tolerant with ourselves.

Listening to our mates' perspectives and opinions with genuine open-mindedness is one way to show tolerance. Sometimes partners will act open-minded, but in reality have no intention of allowing their partners to influence their own points of view. Standing firm in maintaining a belief or opinion felt strongly about is one thing, but close-mindedness to the inputs of others is quite another. The former position is quite admirable; the latter is sad for both mates, as their relationship is likely to remain rigid, with little room for growth.

RES:

Like every married couple, Susan and I have had many conversations in which we've both expressed our personal points of view regarding various topics. As we've shared our opinions about different issues, there have been countless times when it's become obvious to me that my wife has a better idea than I do. When this happens, I've always found it important to communicate it quickly. ("I believe you're right!" "I'm convinced your idea will work better than mine," "You know what? You've talked me into trying your plan," and so forth.)

Letting your companion know when he or she is "right" or has a "better idea" should never be used as some sort of manipulative technique. Acknowledging your own weaknesses and others' strengths is an important principle to apply with anyone you wish to have an honest relationship with. In addition to helping you become more empathetic, this practice also helps both partners quickly focus on any points of agreement between them.

Married people also need to treat themselves with dignity, self-respect, and tolerance. This means communicating clearly that they take their own opinions and feelings seriously.

Sometimes marriage partners think they are in a subordinate position to their mate, and don't feel free to express their opinions in conversations. This pattern may occur for a variety of reasons. The "subdued" spouse may be less articulate in verbal skills; perhaps one mate feels inferior to the other because of differences in educational back-grounds, jobs, or income levels. Or, it might be due to the person's beliefs about the "appropriate" roles of a husband and a wife. Regardless of why this pattern may occur, it is not conducive to a strong and healthy marriage.

In a thriving marriage, both husband and wife believe it's a right and responsibility to com-municate their thoughts and feelings to each other. Thriving partners strive to view and relate to one another on the same plane—not from a superior-sub-ordinate perspective. Whose

Your spouse's opinions should always be considered with great respect.

opinions are more important should never be an issue. Each spouse's opinions and feelings should always be con-sidered with great respect.

Regardless of your previous patterns of communication, we encourage you to adopt a style where you both express your views forthrightly. Show your self-respect by standing up for your own thoughts, opinions, and feelings while respecting your mate by evaluating what he or she says with an open mind. Empathizing with your companion's feelings is one of the most important ways to communicate your sincere desire to understand and support your best friend.

Webster's Dictionary defines empathy as "The power to enter into the feeling or spirit of others." Empathy goes hand-in-hand with the principle of "listen and learn." It is an effective catalyst in helping husbands and wives bridge the gap in their misunderstandings and disagreements. Being empathetic comes easily to some and not so easily to others. Nevertheless, it's an attribute every person can develop. Because it has such a powerful, positive influence on all couples, learning to empathize is certainly a skill worth fostering.

Remember a time you heard someone tell a story, and you identified with the feelings that were described because you had had similar feelings or experiences? You were empathizing with another person. Knowing that you've been able to identify with someone else's feelings, experiences, or opinions is the beginning step to identifying readily with your own spouse.

Empathy is easiest when you've had similar experiences or feelings, but it can also be strengthened by pushing yourself to listen intently for whatever feelings are being shared. Be careful, though, in using the phrase, "I understand how you feel." We often do not truly understand what our mate feels or why he or she feels a certain way. We're usually on safer ground by reflecting what we perceive our mate is feeling in tentative terms: "It seems to me that . . ." "I can see you're really upset," or "It sounds like . . ."

When you don't know exactly how your mate feels, you can acknowledge his or her feelings and express your attempts to understand with statements such as, "Even though I don't know how it feels, I can see it is very difficult for you." This demonstrates your sincere effort to try to understand, acknowledge, and empathize with your spouse's feelings.

4. Clarify What the Real Issues Are

How many times have you been upset, hurt, or angry over something, and have not been exactly sure why? Do you take the time to evaluate what has happened, what you're feeling, and why? Such a self-evaluation is meaningful to clarify what's going on. For example, if you find that you're annoyed when your husband invites his buddies over for "Monday Night Football," ask yourself: "Am I irritated because of the mess they make, or do I mainly resent the time it takes away from the two of us?"

Another aspect of clarifying the issue is determining who "owns" the problem. Sometimes a problem is really not a marital issue, but one that belongs to the husband or wife. Remember, a thriving marriage is a relationship between two mature adults. Each spouse must assume personal responsibility to deal with many personal problems alone. If the way your husband or wife brushes teeth irritates you, it could be that the real problem is yours, and that you need to deal with it—perhaps by leaving the room while he or she is brushing, or changing your attitude to be more tolerant and accepting.

> ### *Three approaches to challenges:*
>
> ✔ *Internal change of attitude.*
> ✔ *Personal action to change behavior.*
> ✔ *Collaborative effort.*

The nature of the problem dictates how we should confront it. Some challenges require an internal change of attitude; others require that we take personal action to correct our own behavior, and still others require a collaborative effort between spouses.

Suppose a continual source of contention in your marriage is being late. To confront this effectively, you need to determine the real issue. In reality, is the lateness a matter of:

- Not planning ahead effectively?
- Cramming too much into a short period of time?
- Indecisiveness or inefficiency?
- Being generally inconsiderate toward others?
- Vindictively "getting back at" the spouse?
- Not having the knowledge or willpower to break old habits?

If both partners are committed to being honest with themselves and each other (an essential requirement for a thriving marriage), they'll quickly get to the root of their problems so they can resolve them and move forward.

In agreeing on the real issues, remember: When attempting to resolve conflicts, it's easy to get off-track with peripheral "stuff." It will help your discussion if you have agreed, up front, what the real issue to resolve is ("So, can we agree that what we're trying to resolve in this discussion is . . ."). When you've done this, if either partner gets off-track during the discussion, the other can appropriately refocus by saying, "Didn't we agree we're discussing . . . ? Afterwards, we'll discuss . . ." It's important to stay focused on the real issue and stick to it until you've agreed on a solution.

5. Work on One Conflict at a Time

Sometimes people who are very bright or talk on a complex level deal with multiple issues in one conversation. Regardless of your intelligence or verbal skills, however, it's usually more effective to stay focused on a single conflict to resolve before moving on to additional ones. Couples also tend to get sidetracked in their conflict resolution efforts with defensiveness and "bottomless-pit digging."

Defensive Reactions

To defend ourselves in a conversation, we often introduce other "stuff," which immediately dilutes the effectiveness of our discussion. We've all been in conversations when someone reacts defensively with "But, what about when you . . ."

> *To avoid being defensive, take the initiative to ask your helpmate for constructive feedback.*

Preventing this reaction between spouses requires a high level of maturity; it is clearly an ideal most of us need to work at continually to realize. To avoid defensiveness, actively ask your helpmate for constructive criticism. You'll be amazed at how much less defensive you feel when drawing upon the useful feedback your mate can provide, rather than reacting defensively to his or her candid efforts to "call it as I see it."

Bottomless-Pit Digging

"Bottomless-pit digging" occurs when one partner is never satisfied with his or her mate's progress. For example, after your spouse has made a significant improvement, you pull out your list of "other things" to work on. This is discouraging, and your spouse may feel you're focusing only on his or her weaknesses. To avoid this, develop the habit of expressing real gratitude for progress made—and then leave it alone. There will be time enough to bring up other areas to work on later.

6. Build upon Points of Agreement

Couples know that not all marital problems can be solved by focusing on a single narrow issue. Some conflicts involve complex issues with several facets. Those experienced in mediating conflict between two parties value the technique of getting both individuals to identify their points of agreement. This works best when applied early in the process, and is especially useful whenever people reach an impasse. This strategy ignites more positive energy between the two of you, putting both of you in a better position to approach—and constructively resolve—any remaining points.

Although it may seem there's no common ground, exploring the foundations of the issue may help clarify where the points of agreement and disagreement lie. It's fairly easy to determine the points of disagreement; after all, that's why you're in the middle of a conflict. A greater challenge is exploring areas where a common thread of agreement can be found. This takes patience and a sincere desire to find an acceptable solution.

> *Identify common threads of agreement as a foundation to build the structure of the final solution.*

Start with the basics of the issue and move backward, if necessary, to the very "core" of your conflict. Once you've identified any points of agreement, you can then concentrate on how to build upon them. This could include negotiating, compromising, and doing whatever "give and take" is needed to resolve any points you don't agree upon.

Suppose a couple decides they'd like to purchase a vehicle. The husband's first inclination is for "a rugged, four-wheel-drive truck," but the wife wants "a nice compact car that's good on mileage." After further discussion they conclude they can agree on the following: a vehicle that drives well in the snow and is reasonably economical. At this point, they're much better prepared to continue a productive discussion and refine their thinking further, until they've reached a conclusion about exactly what they will buy.

7. Stay Solution-Focused

Once engaged in problem-solving, it's easy to focus on the first part of the process and forget the second. While it's necessary to clarify what the problems and conflicts are, both spouses really need to concentrate on the solution, not the problem.

*O*RES:

Years ago, my brother Mark shared something he'd learned while attending business school. One professor indicated that many companies have developed a strongly enforced policy to ensure greater efficiency and effectiveness during their board meetings. Simply stated, the rule is this: "No member is permitted to bring up any problems unless he or she also offers at least one possible solution."

This is now a practice that has been adopted by many organizations and leaders. Thus, in almost any discussion of problems, people are routinely expected to suggest several alternatives and then give their recommended solution.

Marriage partners can learn a useful lesson from the business world. Husbands and wives might choose to adopt the informal policy that any time either spouse has a complaint, he or she needs to offer several solutions for the two of them to discuss.

This approach helps us avoid the habit of "venting" whenever we're bothered about something. We must be proactive in expressing our concerns instead of simply reacting emotionally.

If a couple adopts a solution-centered policy, less time is spent debating—and problems can be resolved more quickly. If either partner slips into a long, drawn-out discussion of grievances and problems, he or she can be gently reminded (humorously, if possible) to discuss the solutions. This simple, non-critical reminder, when offered in the right spirit, quickly restores the discussion to a more productive level.

Sometimes problems are brought up for reasons other than a need to solve them; it may be all our mate needs is a listening ear and an understanding heart. If ever in doubt, simply ask: "Do you want me to just listen, or do you want my recommendations for solutions?" If you want to "vent" frustrations of the day, you can begin your dialogue with, "I want you just to listen."

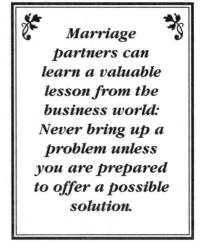

Marriage partners can learn a valuable lesson from the business world: Never bring up a problem unless you are prepared to offer a possible solution.

Naturally, we all have times when we simply don't know how to solve certain problems. When this is the case, we are not in a position to offer any solution at all. These are times when we need our helpmate. We all need to occasionally depend on others, especially our spouse, for suggestions on overcoming those challenges we haven't been able to handle on our own.

8. Ask for Changes That Will Make Things Better

Some people have a habit of readily expressing their negative feelings about virtually everything. Perhaps they learned this from their parents, friends, coworkers, or simply picked it up from the media; it doesn't really matter. What matters is that this practice usually has an undesirable effect on their marriage. Whether this takes the form of complaining, whining, blaming circumstances, or criticizing others, the consequences are similar: Negativity produces more negativity.

Benjamin Franklin said, "Any fool can criticize, condemn, and complain—and most fools do." Those who want to avoid being a "fool" in marriage might heed this simple advice: Don't just complain; ask for a reasonable change that will make the situation better. This goes hand-in-hand with the use of "I" statements. We previously discussed the first two steps of "I" statements: presenting (a) what the problem is and (b) how you feel about it (in a non-threatening way). The third and fourth steps of this process are to (c) ask for a change, and (d) ask how you can help or encourage the desired change.

Step I

Identify the problem or behavior:

"When you continue to leave your clothes in a pile . . ."

Step II

State how you feel about it, or how you react.

". . . I feel like I'm your maid, and I become resentful."

Step III

Ask for a change.

"I would like you to put your clothes in the hamper every time you shower."

Step IV

Ask what you can do to help or encourage the change.

"How can I encourage this?"

Altogether it looks like this: "When you continue to leave your clothes in a pile, I feel like I'm your maid, and I become resentful. I would like you to put your clothes in the hamper every time you shower. How can I encourage this?"

This filters the way you mentally, emotionally and verbally process problems. When you find yourself upset with your helpmate, make it a point to take an additional step. Change your focus from "what I don't like" to "what changes would make it better?" Carefully determine what your mate could do differently to lead to a better outcome. Retrace the steps that led to the undesirable outcome. It might help to visualize your mate doing something differently that leads to a result you feel better about. If possible, communicate the preferred changes using positive terms.

So, rather than saying: "I hate it when you . . ." consider saying: "I'd really like it if you would . . ." Instead of: "It really annoys me every time you . . ." try: "It would mean a lot to me if you would remember to . . ."

This method is not intended as a clever or sneaky way to dictate your mate's behavior. Both husband and wife must always honor each other's agency in responding (or not responding) to the request. Instead, it's a simple way for both partners to treat each other with respect and courtesy. The approach isn't a typical one, but it's sure to make a real difference. You'll be surprised to find that you're

Change your focus from "What I don't like" to "What changes would make it better?"

"bugged" with each other a lot less, and when problems do crop up, they will be handled more efficiently and effectively. This is one habit that's worth spending some time to cultivate—in your marriage and in all your relationships.

9. Apologize and Forgive

Apology and forgiveness are on two sides of the same coin. When we have one, we need the other. Have you ever had problems with either of these cardinal principles of relationships? Maybe you know how to apologize, but find it hard to forgive, or vice versa. It's extremely difficult, as imperfect people living around other imperfect people, when we are incapable of forgiving or apologizing to others—especially our best friends.

"I'm sorry" is the most important two-word sentence in the English language. When expressed honestly and sincerely, it really helps heal relationships. Nothing can soften the heart of one who's been hurt or offended more than a sincere apology; it cannot change what has happened, but it can change the feelings of all involved. Yet we are sometimes reluctant to offer an apology, even when we know we've done something inappropriate. Why?

Admitting we're wrong is difficult when we fear anger, rejection, or punishment. So, instead of admitting we're wrong, we sometimes attempt to blame someone or something, cover it up, or simply lie about it. All individuals need to admit mistakes to themselves; we married persons must also acknowledge our shortcomings and apologize to our mates when we offend them. It's important to avoid apologizing frequently without doing anything to correct our offensive behavior. Such "apologies" are soon viewed by our partners as insincere cop-outs, rather than genuine resolutions to change our ways.

 When offering an apology, make sure you:

> *1. Acknowledge your mistake.*
> *2. Accept personal responsibility.*
> *3. Are sincere.*
> *4. Change behaviors or attitudes.*
> *5. Ask for help and feedback as needed.*

The flip side of this coin is sometimes the hardest of all: learning to forgive our mates or ourselves. When we make mistakes and say, "I'm sorry," we need not only the forgiveness of our spouses, but also the forgiveness of ourselves, with an attempt to redeem our behavior. In turn, we need a forgiving heart for others, especially our companion. We carry a tremendous burden when we choose not to forgive, and the weight of that burden increases with time. It can tear us apart if we're unable to let it go. To be free of grudges or unforgiven hurts is one of the best feelings in the world. There are more than enough burdens to carry in this world, without the additional weight of unforgiven anger or hurt.

> ### *Steps of Forgiveness:*
>
> 1. *Recognize the mistake for what it is: an indication that your spouse is imperfect.*
> 2. *Separate the behavior from the person; your mate still deserves to be loved.*
> 3. *Acknowledge and work through your feelings—then let them go.*
> 4. *Choose to forgive sincerely and completely— as much for yourself as your spouse.*
> 5. *Say the three healing words, "I forgive you"—and mean it.*

10. Seek Mutually Acceptable Solutions

Wisdom dictates that different challenges call for different approaches. Whatever methods a couple uses should include both partners striving to reach a mutually acceptable solution. Of the several methods described below, the first is a common approach we don't recommend. The rest, however, might serve you well, depending on the challenge you're confronting.

Win-Lose

This approach to solving problems is used by many people who feel the need to protect themselves from being "wrong." Thus, the attitude of, "I must win, and you must lose" is created. In some instances, this style is a carryover from the athletic arena, where there's typically only one "winner" in a competition. Unfortunately, in a marriage this orientation reinforces a sense of "opponents" rather than "partners."

It's certainly possible to resolve many problems using the "win-lose" model. However, when spouses get their own way at the expense of their mates, they unwittingly do themselves a great disservice. Though they may get what they want, if their mates feel like they've "lost" (agreed to something they really didn't want), it inevitably undermines their relationship. If a wife goes along with her husband's decision to buy a truck she feels they cannot afford, her resentment will affect other aspects of their interaction. Perhaps she'll start buying things to spite him, avoid conversations altogether, or become secretive. Marriage partners who adopt the "win-lose" model may win the battle of the specific issue, but will lose the war of a quality relationship.

Win-Win

The best way for husbands and wives to resolve conflict is the "win-win" approach, meaning that each person gets what he or she wants from the solution. The solution may be in a different form or package than expected, but each spouse can get what he or she wants. Some who advocate this model claim that when people choose to compromise, they assume it's necessary to divide an existing pie into smaller pieces. In the "win-win" approach, however, the desire is to create a bigger pie for all to share. Partners engaged in win-win resolutions develop stronger relationships because they are equally committed to making these solutions work.

 A Win-Win approach works best when:

✔ ***Issues are too complex or important for compromise.***
✔ ***Conflict levels between spouses are minimal.***
✔ ***The people and problems involved are separate.***

A collaborative, win-win approach to conflict resolution will benefit the marriage of a couple who implements it. In married life, there isn't enough time or energy for a full-blown, collaborative approach to every conflict. Besides, some problems simply aren't worth it. Reality requires that couples must sometimes resolve differences and work through conflicts using an alternative approach; what really matters is that couples do what it takes to solve their problems. As long as a couple can resolve conflict in a reasonable and positive manner, they owe it to themselves to be flexible. What's often called for is compromise.

Compromise

For some people, compromise is a dirty word, typically because it is associated with weakness. But most marriage experts agree that learning how to compromise is a necessary and useful skill. Compromise is the mature, "give and take" approach necessary in all relationships. Couples who understand this can use compromise to their mutual advantage. There are four basic varieties of compromise to consider: *Middle of the Road, Take Turns, Yield,* and *Agree to Disagree.*

A. Middle of the Road

Consider how marriage partners view the spending of money. Perhaps a wife is rather frugal and resists spending money unless absolutely necessary. On the other hand, her husband feels that any cash on hand is burning a hole in his pocket, and uses credit cards as "free money." What should they do?

 A middle-of-the-road approach calls for
both partners to:

✔ *Acknowledge any extremes of attitude or behavior on their part.*
✔ *Recognize the value of their mates' position.*
✔ *Adopt a plan that is somewhere between the two extremes.*

A middle-of-the-road approach calls for both partners to acknowledge any extremes of attitude or behavior on their part, recognize the value of their mates' position, and adopt a plan that is somewhere between the two extremes. For example, the husband might say, "You know, dear, I think you were right about us needing to be more careful with our money," and the wife might respond with, "Yes, sweetheart, but I can see now that you were also right; in order to enjoy life a little more, we need to be willing to spend some of our money on the things we need and enjoy." Both can then focus on how they manage their finances in between the extreme positions previously maintained.

B. Take Turns

The middle-of-the-road approach does not apply to some conflicts. In selecting a shared activity, you can't go to a motocross race and see a movie at the same time. However, the couple can accomplish both "wants" by taking turns. For example: "Since the concert you want to attend is only this Saturday, and the team's in town for two weekends, I'll gladly go to the concert with you, if we can go to the game I want to see next weekend." When using the "taking turns" approach, the goal of compromise is to solve problems equitably. Couples do best when both partners sincerely attempt to be reasonable and fair, rather than compulsively keeping track to ensure that it's always "50-50."

C. Yield

In this form of compromise, one partner decides to "go along" with his or her mate's preference. Perhaps your spouse has convinced you of a better idea, or simply has much stronger feelings than you do about his or her preferences. Maybe you yield simply because your companion has supported you so much, he or she deserves an indulgence. Regardless of the reason, if you choose to go along with your mate's preference, do so willingly. A spouse who claims to have yielded to his or her mate's wishes while complaining or dragging feet isn't really compromising at all. Furthermore, if one marriage partner does most of the yielding, you may not be applying the compromise principle, but have instead slipped into a win-lose pattern.

D. Agree to Disagree

Sometimes, no matter how a conflict is approached, you may never be able to agree on a solution. Under such circumstances, you might apply the *Agree to Disagree* approach. Simply acknowledge to one another that you don't see eye-to-eye. It does not matter whether your opinions are based on important moral beliefs or mere personal preferences. Either way, both marriage partners must fully accept each other's right to their individual views.

When you agree to disagree, you accept your mate's right to exercise his or her agency as an individual with firm opinions. A married couple can disagree without being disagreeable; they can depend on each other as strong individuals with a healthy self-respect. Experienced marriage partners recognize that no two people, including spouses, will agree on every issue—nor should they expect to. As rational adults, we cannot take offense when, despite our best efforts to convince another that we're right, our partner still doesn't see things the way we do. It's natural for husbands and wives to use this form of compromise as a normal part of the conflict resolution process. It's really okay to agree to disagree.

Cautions in Using an "Agree to Disagree" Compromise:

1. *After you've agreed to disagree, if either of you hold resentment toward your spouse—whether harbored inside or expressed vocally—you're out of line. Such a reaction shows you haven't maintained the true spirit of compromise.*

2. *If you find that on most major issues, you almost always "agree to disagree" instead of working out a solution, you might find your paths will drift apart until there is ultimately a major rift in your marriage relationship. Whenever possible, attempt to resolve the conflict or use a form of compromise that brings you together. Particularly when dealing with conflicts over important issues, try to use the "agree to disagree" approach on a very limited basis.*

After you've agreed to disagree, if either of you has a negative attitude or resentment toward your spouse—whether held inside or expressed vocally—you have not maintained the true spirit of compromise. If you find that on most major issues you usually agree to disagree instead of working out an acceptable solution, your paths may keep drifting apart until there is, ultimately, a major rift in your relationship. Whenever possible, try to resolve the conflict or use a form of compromise that brings you together. Particularly when dealing with conflicts over important issues, use the *Agree to Disagree* approach on a very limited basis.

The Edison Principle and More

Some couples are too easily discouraged when they cannot resolve issues quickly. It's easy to think "Gee, we've just spent 45 minutes and haven't gotten anywhere; this was a waste of time—I knew it wouldn't work." Sadly, couples who adopt this attitude rarely resolve conflicts and subsequently pay a major price in their relationship.

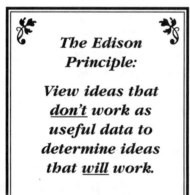

The Edison Principle:

View ideas that don't work as useful data to determine ideas that will work.

The example of Thomas Edison can be instructive to marriage partners. To identify an element that would work as a filament for the incandescent lightbulb, he tried literally thousands of different materials—none of which worked. Yet, he did not feel that he was a failure as an inventor, nor that the scientific method was a failure. Instead, his attitude each time a material proved unsuitable was: "Well, I've discovered one more material that won't work." Couples who don't resolve their conflict after significant effort could adopt a similar attitude: "Well, it looks like we've discovered several more options that aren't going to work for us. Let's approach this another time and we'll know what ideas to disregard while exploring some fresh possibilities!"

Using the Edison principle in conflict resolution means that if, during your *Resolve* sessions, you haven't been able to arrive at a mutually acceptable solution, you don't give up. View any unacceptable options as additional data that you know won't work. Reschedule a specific, future time when you can both "go at it" again, knowing you'll need to evaluate different possibilities together. Your time has not been wasted, but used in the process of determining what solutions will not be mutually acceptable.

Open-Mindedness and Brainstorming

It's easy for couples to get "bogged down" when either spouse has the attitude that there is a "right" or "wrong" way to do things. This stubborn, narrow thinking happens when two individuals lock themselves in a debate over which of two opinions is better. It is unnecessary. In reality, there are often many possible solutions, any one of which might work. Both persons need to become more open-minded in the way they view alternative solutions to problems.

One creative solution to breaking out of an impasse is quite simple: brainstorming. Brainstorming can work just as well in marriage as it can to help a committee decide on a logo. Unfortunately, marriage partners don't use this method very often to resolve conflicts. If you and your mate find yourselves stuck in a deadlock, follow the two simple guidelines for brainstorming: (1) generate several possible solutions without critiquing, discussing, or evaluating; (2) review your list of possibilities one by one, evaluating each to determine which you agree would be best.

Brainstorm to break through times when you're "stuck."

By approaching this task as a fun, free-wheeling adventure to work through your challenges, you'll find you have an entirely different experience in solving even tough problems. Who knows? You may discover that resolving conflicts in marriage can feel less like weary warriors fighting it out and more like enthusiastic adventurers taking on a mountain!

Ensuring Understanding and Follow-Through

Once you have resolved your conflict in a way that's mutually acceptable, take two final, easy steps to ensure success:

1. Summarize exactly what it is you've agreed upon: "Do we agree, then, that you will not bring up my diet in conversations with others?"
2. Reconfirm any commitments to follow-through: "So, starting this week, I'm going to take the kids to their practices, and you're going to help them each night with their math, right?"

MAIN IDEAS:
Resolve

Differences between mates are normal, so it's useful to accept each other and focus on ways they can help you.

Guidelines to resolve conflict as a couple:

1. Promptly and regularly resolve conflicts.
2. Listen and learn.
3. Be patient, tolerant, and empathetic.
4. Clarify what the real issues are.
5. Work on one conflict at a time.
6. Build upon points of agreement.
7. Stay solution-focused.
8. Ask for a change.
9. Apologize and forgive.
10. Seek mutually acceptable solutions.
  - Apply the Edison Principle to move from discouragement to hope.
  - Brainstorm to reinforce open-mindedness and enthusiasm, generate possible solutions, and break through impasses.
  - Ensure successful implementation of solutions by summarizing agreements and confirming commitments to follow through.

20 QUESTIONS
to Ponder and Discuss:

First, ask yourself the following questions about how you and your helpmate resolve challenges. Then discuss these questions with your spouse by asking: "How am I doing?" and "How might we improve?"

1. Do I accept our differences as a natural part of life and marriage, or view them as evidence that there's something "wrong" with my mate or our relationship?
2. Do I view the differences between us as opportunities to complement each other's weaknesses and strengthen our marriage?
3. Have I tried to learn constructive ways to better understand and deal with our differences?
4. If our time together is limited, have we determined what we can do to spend more of it in ways that are pleasant and positive?
5. Have we established a regular weekly time (a *Resolve* session) to discuss our challenges and resolve our conflicts?
6. Do I use "active listening" to understand my mate's viewpoints and communicate effectively?
7. Am I open-minded and willing to change my personal perspective if it seems appropriate?
8. Do I understand my spouse's feelings and show emotional support?
9. Do I focus on identifying the real issues early in our discussions? Do I assume responsibility for my own problems, rather than burden my mate with them?
10. Do I stick with one issue at a time, and avoid getting sidetracked? Could I be less defensive by proactively seeking constructive criticism from my spouse?
11. Could I help work through our disagreements more effectively by identifying and building on our points of agreement?

12. When I'm upset with my spouse, do I focus on solving the problem, rather than talking about the problem?
13. Do I ask for reasonable changes that will make the situation better, rather than complain or criticize?
14. Can I do a better job of apologizing when I have offended my spouse, and of demonstrating the sincerity of my apology by improving my behavior?
15. When I have had my feelings hurt, do I forgive him or her, rather than holding on to resentment or bitter feelings?
16. Have I learned to effectively apply collaboration and compromise to reach mutually acceptable solutions?
17. The next time we fail to reach consensus, can we apply the *Edison Principle* to restore perspective, and then schedule another time to explore different alternatives?
18. When I find myself locked in an impasse with my spouse, can we brainstorm to resolve our conflicts and "lighten up" the process?
19. Do I verbally summarize what we have agreed upon and confirm who is going to do what?
20. What else have I learned about the *Resolve* practice (outside of this book) that I can apply to our benefit?

Now What?

After evaluating where you are in this practice, use the *KISS Marriage Maker*™ to identify goals to improve those areas which need help. You might want to concentrate on one area at a time for a week or two, then move on to another area. This could be an effective way to specifically improve and see the results of your effort.

RESOLVE:
Ideas to Consider

The following ideas can help you focus on specific things you can do to deal with differences and resolve conflicts in your marriage.

- List several differences between you and your mate. Identify one way each difference can benefit you individually and in your marriage.
- Make it a rule that neither of you will resort to name-calling, blaming, or criticizing.
- Listen to your spouse without interrupting and then reflect back what he or she says to make sure you understand.
- Pick a regular time each week to confront and resolve your issues and challenges.
- Mark the time for these *Resolve* sessions on your calendars.
- Together, discuss a communication book you have read or tape series you've listened to.
- Attend a communication training course together.
- Cultivate open-mindedness by telling your mate you are eager to try out new suggestions.
- When resolving issues, first identify a single challenge to resolve, and remain focused on resolving that one issue.
- When upset about something, describe how you would like it to be different (instead of what it is you don't like).
- Rather than complain or criticize, ask your spouse for a specific, reasonable change that will make the situation better.
- If you've offended your mate or hurt feelings, apologize sincerely, and then take steps to improve your behavior.

- Reflect on whether you might be harboring resentment toward your mate. If so, take the initiative to forgive him or her.
- Frequently say to your mate, "Let's make sure we come up with a solution we both feel good about."
- When resolving a conflict, briefly review the four varieties of compromise and determine if any one might offer a good solution: *Middle of the Road, Take Turns, Yield, Agree to Disagree.*
- If discouraged when you don't resolve an issue, apply the *Edison Principle* and try again another time, considering different alternatives.
- When locked in an impasse, use brainstorming to generate five possible solutions to a problem, then pick the top two.
- Once you have agreed upon a solution, verbally confirm what the decision is and who will do what kind of follow-up.

"The dogmas of the quiet past are inadequate for the stormy present and future. As our circumstances are new, we must think anew, and act anew."

— *Abraham Lincoln* —

GROW

Refine the Shared Vision and
Spousal Synergy
with Your Life Partner

ℋAVE YOU ever asked yourself, "Why are we working so hard at our marriage?" or "What's all this about, anyway?" Although we're not prepared to address the full "meaning of life" question, we do want to focus on the potential every marriage relationship can have.

Remember this dialogue between Alice and the Cheshire Cat in *Alice in Wonderland?*

Alice: "Am I on the right road?"
Cheshire Cat: "Well, where are you going?"
Alice: "I'm not quite sure."
Cheshire Cat: "Then, any road will do."

As couples on the Marriage Highway, you need to decide where you want to go and what you want from your relationship. Because, unless you know what you want—both in terms of a destination and how you want your journey to go—any road will do, any partner will do, and any haphazard way you choose to get there will do.

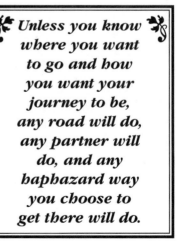

> *Unless you know where you want to go and how you want your journey to be, any road will do, any partner will do, and any haphazard way you choose to get there will do.*

For those who know the kind of relationship they want, the path is clear. It is marked by the principles and practices outlined in this book and culminates with the goals, dreams and vision the two of you have defined together. It can last a few years or a lifetime; you choose. The investment of time and energy you put into it will determine not only the length of your journey, but also the joy or misery you'll experience along the way.

This chapter will take you beyond the moments of frustration and joy, sadness and laughter, failures and triumphs. It will open your eyes to the potential you share as lifelong companions—living and growing together. It will help you understand that our daily struggles and successes are the process to help us become better individuals and have the type of relationship wherein we want to be together forever!

The *Grow* practice is a hallmark that distinguishes thriving marriages from merely surviving ones. Even when partners do well with the other five practices, unless they continually grow as life partners, they'll fall short of a great marriage. In other words, it's quite possible for a man and woman to share common interests, treat one another with kindness and respect, communicate, have a great sex life, confront their conflicts, and be skilled at solving problems. Nevertheless, these are not enough. All are necessary but insufficient for those who have a higher goal in mind. This is somewhat ironic, because couples who apply the first five practices are, in a very real way, growing in their marriage; they just haven't developed a vision of where they're going.

For example, every time a couple successfully confronts and resolves a conflict, they have grown. Not only have they improved their relationship from where it was, they've also strengthened their ability to deal with future challenges. These practices will help couples weather their storms, and perhaps even feel that they're "getting along just fine." Yet, without growth, something vitally important will be lacking. A thriving marriage requires two partners fully engaged in life. This is not an end result, but an ongoing process in which each spouse continually refines his or her

efforts. Besides relating to each other positively, purpose-
fully, and passionately, everyone does best when he or she
masters the art of personal and couple growth. When both
marriage partners grow—as individuals and as a couple—
both want to remain partners for life, and beyond.

This chapter focuses on two critical dimensions of what
it takes to grow in marriage: refining your shared vision and
creating spousal synergy. But first we shall briefly introduce
an important concept underlying both of these dimensions.

We Versus Me

Self-sufficiency and competitiveness are traits that have
been strongly reinforced in Western culture. Although
there are several important benefits of these characteristics,
they also create significant problems—particularly in marriage, where cooperation and interdependence are far
more useful than competition.

$\mathscr{O}$RES:

> I always enjoyed the humorous way the battle of
> the sexes was depicted in the musical *Annie Get Your
> Gun.* In one memorable scene, Annie Oakley and her
> male counterpart verbally "duke it out" in the musical
> duet: "Anything You Can Do, I Can Do Better!"
>
> If they have learned how to work together, when
> a husband and wife are striving to grow and realize
> their full potential, it's generally more productive
> when they adopt a variation on that song: "Anything
> I Can Do, *We* Can Do Better!"

Social commentators have noted that the self-centered
"me generation" has experientially discovered that it makes
much more sense to become the "we generation." Though a
"we" orientation may be helpful in any organization or social
institution, it's absolutely essential for spouses who hope to
be thriving life partners. Many individuals have learned that
they achieve superior results when they cooperate, rather

than compete. Unfortunately, lots of folks give lip service to the concept of interdependence, whereas few really apply it effectively in their own marriage. This chapter will provide life partners with both reasons and methods to use shared vision and spousal synergy to grow interdependently.

Shared Vision

To understand the *Grow* practice, which is primarily positive, it's necessary to touch on a slightly negative aspect of growth. "We just grew apart" is a phrase used by some to describe how and why their marriage has died. In effect, what "we grew apart" usually means is: (a) One spouse grew and the other didn't progress, stay interesting, or remain connected to his or her mate's development; or (b) although each partner may have grown as an individual, the relationship remained stagnant. This is very different from what happens in a thriving marriage. When a husband and wife are committed to growing in their relationship, they feel like they are real partners, and they very much enjoy their journey in life together.

Stagnation, or simply doing nothing, is not a static condition; not in ponds, not in one's personal life, and certainly not in marriage. Some people mistakenly view marriage as though it were a sterile institution. But, in reality, marriage is a dynamic set of complex, ever-changing relationships—each with a life of its own. Therefore, if a couple makes no effort to change or improve their marriage, it will not simply remain unchanged. Instead, it will begin to deteriorate and will eventually die. In some respects, it's irrelevant whether or not a couple have legally divorced; if spouses have divorced emotionally, the effects on their lives and hearts can be very similar to those that

> *If spouses have emotionally divorced, the effects in their hearts and lives can be very similar to those that occur when a marriage officially ends.*

occur when a marriage officially ends. In our personal development, if we are not growing, we are withering and dying. In our marriage relationships, either we are growing forward or sliding backward.

What leads some marriages to grow and others to stagnate? One key is explained in this pronouncement from Solomon, found in Proverbs 29:18: "Where there is no vision, the people perish . . ." The same could be said for marriage partners who fail to develop a shared vision. Unless they determine what it is they really want and what it is they truly believe in, marriage partners tend to merely meander—perhaps together, perhaps alone.

It's easy for spouses to drift apart if they do not chart a course together to give their lives shared meaning. Without unity and direction, how can partners possibly stay on the same track? This is an even bigger dilemma in today's world than it used to be. We're bombarded by options like never before, and there are many voices beckoning us to follow one path or another in how we conduct our lives or carry out our relationships. It's understandable that many husbands and wives would flounder in confusion. They may go through the motions of marriage, but neither feels real movement or momentum in their relationship.

Yet many couples still live their lives almost as separate individuals rather than as real life partners, even when neither spouse is confused or passively indifferent. Each individual in this type of marriage gets so caught up in personal pursuits, that instead of working together as partners, the couple eventually doesn't need each other at all. They become virtual strangers—only connecting with one another superficially.

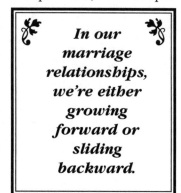

In our marriage relationships, we're either growing forward or sliding backward.

Nevertheless, there is hope. Neither of these outcomes is necessary. The ills of indifference and isolation in marriage are preventable and treatable. To prevent or cure indifference, couples need to develop a shared vision. To avoid the problem of isolation—or to heal it—the couple must learn to relate to one another using spousal synergy. On a simple level, shared vision can be viewed as the "what," and spousal synergy as the "how," for couples to grow in marriage. In other words, shared *vision* consists of mutual goals for the marriage, while spousal *synergy* is the process of working together to achieve these goals.

To develop a shared vision, a husband and wife need to define what they want out of life. This includes a carefully thought-out set of personal objectives, goals for their marriage relationship, and expectations they have for each other. To give this process the attention it deserves will take some time. However, it should not be viewed as a chore. Rather, it's a unique opportunity to shape the direction your lives will take. To do so is to make an investment that yields immense dividends. It's your life that you're planning—as individuals and a couple—so why not make it just as you'd like it to be?

There is no single best way to accomplish this task. Some prefer to approach it as a comprehensive game plan for life; others would rather do it in small, simple ways. In light of what you know about yourself, use your own judgment to determine what will work best for you. In developing a sense of shared vision for your marriage, consider these guidelines:

 Guidelines for Couples to Develop a Shared Vision.

✓ **Develop a Marital Mission Statement.**
✓ **Begin Where You Are.**
✓ **Consider "A Time and a Season."**
✓ **Analyze and Prioritize.**
✓ **Establish Goals and Objectives.**

Develop a Marital Mission Statement

For several years, companies and organizations have found it very beneficial to develop mission statements and vision statements. This single practice has proven invaluable in helping clients and employees clearly understand the organization's primary purpose. A clear, mutual understanding improves unity and helps keep everyone's efforts focused. Many families have also discovered the benefit of developing Family Mission Statements. Whether or not they have children, couples should develop their own Marital Mission Statement.

A Marital Mission Statement can be long and complex, or short and simple. More important is the reason you're writing it. Consistent with the model used in the corporate world, a Marital Mission Statement should express the core beliefs, values, and philosophy of the couple writing it. When major decisions need to be made, it's important to evaluate alternative solutions in light of the mission statement. This will help keep both of you on the road to your goals, within the framework of your beliefs and values.

RES:

Just like each of you, Susan and I are moving along our own Marriage Highway—learning, growing and sometimes stumbling as we go. In spite of life's never-ending challenges, we concentrate on finding joy in our personal lives and in our relationship with each other.

The best brief explanation for our existence we ever found is this statement: "Man and woman are that they might have joy." Using this as our foundation, we wrote our own Marital Mission Statement:

Experiencing joy is the driving force and chief characteristic of our relationship. We seek to recognize and cultivate joyful moments in our daily lives. A primary reason we chose to join our lives as partners in marriage is because we believe each of us will experience more joy together than we ever could as separate individuals. We strive to nurture a continually growing relationship, which we hope will become an eternal marriage. We treat each other in ways that make us not only want to be together, but that will earn us the right to be together forever. We thoroughly enjoy relating to one another as Chosen Companions, Beloved Soulmates, Helpmates, and Eternal Partners.

This is the condensed version of our Marital Mission Statement:

We Are Married That We Might Have Joy in Our Lives.

Here's one way we used this concept: When Susan and I got married, we decided it would be more enjoyable for all concerned to have a fun, informal celebration rather than a formal reception. In addition to having plenty of dancing—a "must" for us—we even had the guests write whatever "words of wisdom" they chose in colorful crayons on our butcher paper-covered round tables! We called it our "Celebration of Joy." We even included a brief excerpt of our Marital Mission Statement in the invitation.

Writing your own Marital Mission Statement will help you clarify what you want out of your core relationship in life. By displaying it prominently where you can refer to it often, it will serve as a continual reminder of your principal pursuits as life partners.

Begin Where You Are

Some couples may get discouraged when thinking about trying to grow in their marriage; they've got their hands full just trying to "hang on." Others might be doing quite well in their marriage, but want to find an effective way they can take their relationship to new heights. It doesn't really matter what kind of journey you have previously had along your Marriage Highway, nor where you currently are. What matters is what you are doing about your journey now.

Wherever we might be on our Marriage Highway, every couple can always find ways to improve. The ideas in this chapter will help you move from where you are to where you'd like to be. Don't be discouraged or give up too soon; any progress the two of you make, however small it might seem, is movement in the right direction. Every effort you make counts. Those who diligently persist find it's the cumulative effect of their ongoing efforts that leads to a major breakthrough and real success.

For example, say you have established a goal to have more harmony in your marriage. Every day that goes by without fighting or yelling indicates progress toward your larger goal. We all have setbacks. If you slip and find yourselves bickering, don't get discouraged and give up.

The *Grow* practice helps couples move from where they are to where they would like to be.

The mere fact that you caught yourselves in an undesirable behavior pattern is another indication that you have grown.

Consider "A Time and a Season"

One concept related to shared vision is expressed quite well in the Bibilical "Ecclesiastes": "To every thing there is a season, and a time to every purpose . . ." There are different seasons throughout the course of all marriages. Throughout history, in every society, couples have had to deal with changing realities and evolving needs at different stages of their lives together. In spite of their unique differences, there are some parallel, almost predictable changes couples face at certain stages of their marriage. For example, the needs may be more similar than different among married persons who are: striving to complete a college degree or vocational training program, involved in pregnancy or childbirth for the first time, adjusting to the demands of a highly dependent infant or toddler, trying to support school-age children or teens in various activities, transitioning to an "empty nest" marriage, making choices and adaptations with career changes, adjusting to limitations imposed by medical or health-related challenges, and so on. Thus, couples do themselves a great service when they learn all they can about such developmental changes. That way they can handle them more effectively.

In some ways—even more than in Dickens' times—our era could be considered "the best of times and the worst of times." We are all aware of the increased stress couples face today. On the other hand, one of the benefits of our times is our increased awareness of the many options available to us. No couple needs to limit themselves to some cookie cutter, "one timetable fits all" formula for what they want from their marriage and when they can pursue it. For example, some young adults get married right out of high school and want to begin rearing children right away, while other couples use medical technology to conceive children when both partners are over forty.

In spite of the many options, however, it's usually helpful when couples carefully consider the time and season of their lives when determining what they want in their marriage. To increase the joy we'll experience in our journey along our Marriage Highway, each of us needs to think about what makes the most sense to us—both as individuals and as partners in a happy and enduring marriage relationship.

In addition to seasonal needs, couples must anticipate circumstances that are not necessarily predictable. Such circumstances are more frequent than ever in our complex, contemporary society. Consider, for example, how the times and seasons of a marriage might be impacted by the following circumstances:

- A husband and wife with a twenty-year age difference, where both have been married several times before.
- A young couple, both college students, with three small children to raise in an interracial marriage.
- A military couple adjusting to the realities of extended absences.
- A retired couple dealing with aging parents and a single-parent adult child living in their home.

There are endless variations in our circumstances. Every couple needs to carefully consider the unique conditions of their own time and season of marriage to best determine their current and future expectations. Taking into account the times and seasons of our lives is important, but we should never forget that we are always accountable for making whatever decisions we need to in order to maintain control of our lives. There are always many choices we can make in any given situation. As with so many options couples can choose, the following are not examples of right or wrong choices, but simply alternatives selected in light of personal views about their own particular time and season.

For example, after this kind of self-evaluation, the young parents in college may determine that inasmuch as they've brought these children into their family by choice, they would prefer to reap more of the benefits of parenting—for themselves and their children—by focusing more time on their family life and less time in preparing for careers. Thus, they might choose to take a more comfortable part-time academic load—even though it means taking a couple of extra years to graduate, rather than living a more pressured lifestyle, which might include having their infants in daycare much of the time. Conversely, the retired couple may determine that they have already spent most of their married years caring for others, and the last few years of their lives is their season to enjoy more as a couple. Thus, their decision could be to care for their aging parents by selecting a quality convalescent center. Furthermore, they may determine that they will allow their daughter and grandchild to live in their home for a six-month period, while she finds a way to become self-supporting and assume the full responsibility to care for her own child—appropriate for her own time and season of being a parent in life.

Analyze and Prioritize

To carefully evaluate a relationship is not a simple process. Neither is it something that can be done "once and for all." A couple hoping to analyze their relationship and establish plans for their entire marriage in one sitting is as unrealistic as the key management team of a company expecting to establish appropriate goals for the lifespan of their organization in a single meeting. Couples must continually reassess how they can meet their ever-changing realities in light of their evolvement as individuals and married persons. To enjoy their journey, couples should take stock of their relationship periodically—at least once a year.

Rather than waiting until the neglected stresses of life seriously damage their marriage (such as occurs during a midlife crisis), savvy partners stage something like purposive "midlife, early-life or late-life crises" and use these times of intentional, holistic reflection as opportunities to reevaluate where they are and what is needed to get where they want to be. (In their excellent book, *Lifebalance*, Linda and Richard Eyre encourage people to have a "Well-Managed Mid-Life Crisis on Purpose.") Shared vision and spousal synergy are not one-time goals that a couple can establish and achieve. Rather, they are ongoing processes that we as partners must continually refine.

Thriving partners are always growing in one way or another—often in several ways simultaneously. For purposive development, each mate must carefully consider what he or she would like to accomplish. This helps the couple to establish realistic goals and specific objectives. We need to think about our overall purpose as we consider where we actually are in our relationship and what our current and upcoming stages of life will bring.

Some couples have the perspective "As long as we're going to spend time evaluating our marriage relationship, why not use this process to discuss our personal growth as well?" Such individuals consider this investment of time and energy in their relationship not as a tedious task, but as an excellent opportunity to discuss matters of personal importance with their very best friend. With this in mind, each spouse might choose to take a fairly comprehensive look at his or her overall personal development as a balanced human being.

So, what do you do once you've analyzed your marriage and perhaps your personal development, as well?

Prioritize what matters most to you as a separate person and as a committed partner. Determine what you want more of in your relationship so you can determine what you want to do less. (Of the many books written on setting priorities, *First Things First,* by Stephen R. Covey, Roger Merrill, and Rebecca Merrill, is one of the best.) As couples establish priorities, they also need to consider the matter of how they grow best. In other words, are they likely to do better by making improvements little by little, or are they more likely to thrive by adopting a more aggressive approach? Remember, there is no right or wrong way to approach this issue. This is totally a matter of how well the partners know themselves and what works best. Regardless of what priorities you establish or what level of intensity works best for you, you'll discover that this process will help you evaluate your many options more effectively. That way you can establish clear goals and specific objectives and achieve them through focused mutual effort.

Establish Goals and Objectives

When developing a shared vision in your marriage, there's a place for both goals and objectives. In either case, clearly define what you want—both for your marriage and from each other as partners.

Goals can be general in nature; our goals might be things we wish for or would like to happen. For example, some couples might have marriage goals such as:

- Always treat each other with kindness and respect.
- Spend more time doing things with other couples.
- Read and discuss good books together.
- Show more affection with lots of hugs and "I love you's."
- Go on a cruise together.
- Take a ten-day backpacking trip together.
- Learn to trust each other more completely.

Objectives are different. They are much more specific in defining precisely what the couple wants to do, acquire, or become, and when they will accomplish these things. When couples establish objectives, they are more likely to see these desires not as something merely hoped for, but as clear outcomes they have committed themselves to accomplishing within a certain time frame.

RES:

My first experience establishing marital objectives was a class assignment in a Personal and Family Finance college course. During the fall of my senior year, a professor asked my class to set five-year goals for ourselves. Being a rather ambitious young man who had been taught by my father that "anything you can conceive and believe, you can achieve," I decided I might as well shoot for what I really wanted to do, in spite of some rather tough obstacles. At the time, in addition to supporting myself entirely in college, I did not own a car, and I was living in the cheapest available basement apartment in town. I was twenty-three years of age and about to get engaged, so I figured I should be clear with my almost-fiancee about my educational, career, and temporal objectives which would significantly impact our next five years together. These were my five-year goals:

1. Complete a bachelor's degree.
2. Complete a master's degree.
3. Complete a doctorate.
4. Be a university professor.
5. Be a marriage and family counselor.
6. Have at least two children.
7. Be out of debt.
8. Own a home.

Actually, these were more personal objectives than they were marital objectives. Nevertheless, I established them at this stage of my life because I knew that to accomplish them would require the full cooperation of a marriage partner. My fiancee probably felt those plans were a bit ambitious, but basically said, "Okay, let's go for it." Exactly five years from that date we had accomplished all the goals except for number 8, because we knew we would be moving in less than a year, and decided to wait until we moved before purchasing a home—which we did ten months later.

It required immense self-discipline and sacrifice to accomplish these objectives, but we both felt that the prize was worth the price, so our tradeoffs seemed worthwhile. We did not feel deprived because we were pursuing goals we had freely chosen.

We all know our goals and objectives don't just happen; we must do something to make them happen. Once you've established mutual goals and objectives, you need to determine specific actions to accomplish them. To do this, list a goal or objective and then list each step or action needed to accomplish the goal. If a specific time frame is involved, it's important to list a date of accomplishment for each action so you can stay on schedule.

𝒮USAN:

In my college classes, I have taught students the following simple format for establishing Objectives and Action Plans:

I. Determine an objective

  A. Define specific actions to accomplish the objective, making sure to address:

    1. Time frame.

    2. Who is responsible.

    3. How we will follow through to ensure it is done.

Here's an example of how a couple can achieve their desire to experience a special shared activity (Objective I) by establishing specific Action Plans:

I. Go on a cruise together in November.

  A. Get brochures and prices from travel agent.

    1. By July 1st.

    2. John.

    3. Linda will check with John on June 15th.

  B. Decide where to go.

    1. By August 15th.

    2. John and Linda will talk with friends who have gone.

3. Discuss and make final decision when out for dinner in mid-August.
C. Save money for trip.
   1. By August 31st.
   2. John and Linda will work on budget and savings plan.
   3. During weekly Marriage Council meeting.
D. Schedule trip for November.
   1. By Sept 7th.
   2. John will book trip with travel agent.
   3. During weekly Marriage Council meeting on September 4th.
E. Board the cruise ship.
   1. During mid-November.
   2. John and Susan.
   3. By remembering to Enjoy the Journey each day of our trip!

Experience teaches us that some things in life we can determine, and others we cannot. When we have specific objectives to accomplish, we must understand and define what we need to do in order to achieve them, and then be willing to work together. This can be easier when we develop written action plans to guide our efforts and ensure they're more effective. Couples who want their lives guided by their Shared Vision need to determine which aspects of this vision are "dreams we'll work for" and which are "objectives we shall accomplish."

𝒮USAN:

Last year, my daughter and son-in-law began a demanding but exciting adventure together. They entered the Amway business and soon were exposed to an organization which required them to think about and develop a Shared Vision of where they wanted to be in five years. This review of their lives included establishing personal and marriage goals. This process has helped them make such positive changes in their lives! Not only have they set goals, they are taking the steps necessary to reach them. They're spending almost as much time in the pursuit of knowledge—gaining new perspectives and learning from books and tapes—as they are in working on their business. Not only are they gleaning ideas about how to build a successful business, but they are learning many practical tips about reinforcing positive marriage and family relationships. I have been so impressed with the personal progress they've made, and also by how their focus on working together toward their mutual goals has brought them closer together.

Once you have established some specific goals and objectives, you will need to periodically review them to ensure they remain consistent with the overall priorities in your lives.

Spousal Synergy

In order to maximize our progress, we need to translate our Shared Vision into effective action. Just as meaningful marital goals are best established by both husband and wife, carrying out their plans also requires a joint effort.

Synergy occurs when the combined efforts of several individuals exceed the total output when those efforts are performed separately. Spousal synergy occurs when a husband and wife apply this concept in their relationship. To understand why and how this can be, consider the following: When we undertake any endeavor, it's always a good idea to determine what resources are available to help us accomplish the task. In the business world, savvy companies recognize that among all the resources they need to accomplish their purposes, it's usually the "human resources"—the people who work for the company—that are most critical.

Most accomplishments do not occur as the result of one person working in isolation. Even when great achievements may be primarily the work of one person, usually this individual can realize the highest level of productivity with the support of some other significant person. This could be a mentor (to show you the ropes in business or education), a coach or teacher (to help athletes or performers refine their craft), an "angel" (the term used for those who provide capital for entrepreneurs during the start-up phases of launching a business enterprise), or a family member.

Suppose that, to find the right kind of person to support you in your personal development and as a marriage partner, you placed an ad including the job description for such an individual. It might look like this:

• WANTED •

Someone to provide support, encouragement, and motivation as I work on becoming the best "Me" I can possibly be in my personal life and in my marriage. Must be able to provide constructive criticism and other forms of feedback in a way that I will feel helped—not "put down." Position requires one who will be very patient with my weaknesses, yet knows how to inspire me to continue striving to become better and better. Needs to be persistent in helping me remember my goals, the progress I've made, and my potential for growth during times when I might become discouraged. Will help me refocus and stay on track when I slip back into old habits. Must be someone I like and care about—an individual I'll work hard to please and won't want to disappoint. As one who is absolutely committed to my growth and development, this person simply will not let me fail in this, the most important endeavor of my life.

Here's the good news: The ideal person to fulfill this job description is your marriage partner. Whether or not your husband or wife is currently skilled in these areas is unimportant. He or she is potentially the very best person for the job. As our best friend, soulmate, and helpmate, our spouse is best suited to be our partner for life—our life partner. In reality, our own husband or wife is the most important human among all "human resources" available to us, as well as the most significant "significant other" to help us realize our potential. This is true for personal goals as well as marriage goals. Our spouse is—at least theoretically—the one person on the planet who is best positioned to help us grow into the person we want to become. So why doesn't this happen more often?

Usually it's one of two reasons: (1) The marriage is more in a "survival" mode rather than a "thriving" mode—mainly because the partners need to do a better job of applying the other five practices, or (2) the spouses have never really understood the *Grow* practice, much less the incredible benefits they could enjoy by applying it. However, once this sinks in and we both really get the picture, there's no end to how we can begin to synergize with each other! We should keep in mind that personal responsibility is always the first order of business. If we want to achieve a goal, we must first make a personal commitment to do whatever it takes to accomplish that objective. Afterwards, it's appropriate to solicit support from our helpmate. Two examples illustrate how to communicate this to a spouse:

1. "I want to work on becoming more mature in the way I handle my personal frustrations. There are several things I can do on my own, but I could really use some support from you. Would you be willing to help me?"

2. "I'm committed to eating more nutritiously. I think my progress would go much faster if we worked on this together. How would you feel about joining me in this endeavor?"

A caution to keep in mind with the *Grow* practice: Sometimes in our zeal to help our mate grow, we can lose sight of a core principle which is fundamental to anyone's development: personal "agency"—the right of every individual to make personal choices and direct his or her own life. Each person should make his or her own decisions about what areas the person might like to improve in life. No adult wants to feel that he or she has become a spouse's "project." It's essential that each mate be shown the dignity and respect of making personal decisions about his or her growth. A failure to do this guarantees that both husband and wife will have a negative experience.

Once a man and woman have agreed to truly support one another in their desires to grow, they may want to consider several ways to mobilize spousal synergy in the relationship. Some of these ways were explained earlier in the book. Hopefully, this will help you see how the same basic concepts can be applied to the *Grow* practice in ways that can yield dividends at an even higher level of return.

 Ways Couples Can Enhance Spousal Synergy:

✓ **Be Effective Sounding Boards.**
✓ **Take Advantage of Feedback.**
✓ **Practice New Behaviors on One Another.**
✓ **Focus on Complementarity.**
✓ **Become Creative Catalysts.**

Be Effective Sounding Boards

As you strive to develop your spousal synergy, a fairly easy place to begin is learning how to be a sounding board for your mate. When problem-solving, it helps to run ideas by another person. Being an effective sounding board basically means listening thoughtfully to your mate while he or she expresses ideas and feelings about something the person cares about.

Sometimes, all your partner really wants is a listening ear to help think aloud or sort through his or her thoughts. On other occasions, your mate may want you to offer your own reaction or personal perspective on the matter. (Here's a good place to use the "Platinum Rule" to determine what kind of sounding board role they would like you to play in supporting them.) If in doubt, always ask, "Do you just want me to listen, or would you rather have me give you advice or ideas on how to resolve your concern?"

Take Advantage of Feedback

Those committed to excellence know it requires feedback from others, because no matter how carefully we scrutinize our own weaknesses, we simply cannot see everything about ourselves—much less know how to correct it. This is why athletes benefit from coaches and musicians from teachers. It's why writers need editors to critique their work and why organizations need to conduct market research and solicit feedback from employees, clients, and consultants. To improve, we need to see how others see us. We can all greatly benefit from different viewpoints and the feedback available from other people.

Our marriage partner is in a position to know us better than anyone else. Living with us on a daily basis, year after year, our mate sees the way we act and react, how we pursue our dreams or procrastinate our responsibilities, the way we express or hold back our positive and negative emotions, what we do when disappointed or happy, the way we handle difficult challenges, unexpected bad news, stressful crises, and moments of triumph. In short, our husband or wife sees us at our best and worst. Individuals who choose to do so can always find ways to hide different facets of who they really are from friends, co-workers, and others. But this is much harder to do with the person we spend our lives with. That's why a mate's feedback can be especially valuable.

> **Those committed to excellence can benefit by soliciting feedback from the one person who knows them better than anyone else—their life partner.**

Unfortunately, the extensive knowledge spouses have about each other is rarely used in constructive ways. Much more commonly, husbands and wives use their awareness destructively—taking potshots at one another, criticizing each other openly, complaining to others about their mate's shortcomings, and so on. How sad for both! The key to making feedback in marriage beneficial is for each spouse to personally cultivate traits of maturity and sensitivity, and for both to nurture mutual respect and trust in their relationship. When the individuals in a marriage have internalized these attributes, it's quite remarkable how much more both can realize their potential. Mature adults will seek their mate's honest feedback, and a sensitive spouse will offer feedback with candor and kindness. Neither would think of saying things in an offensive or hurtful way; after all, this is their very best friend. Because they trust one another completely, we know they can count on each other for feedback intended to be helpful and supportive—not undermining or judgmental of our beloved companion.

Remember, giving and receiving feedback is an art requiring skill and practice—especially during the early phases of our learning. Until both spouses are confident and comfortable receiving feedback, it's best to follow this simple rule of thumb: Feedback should be offered only upon invitation; don't give feedback unless asked to. Couples committed to maximizing their growth and development have no limit as to what areas they can give each other feedback about, when such feedback is wanted. You may want to review "Request Permission to Discuss Challenges" in Chapter 5.

This can be done constructively in many different ways. For feedback to be effective in marriage, each person should use a style that is comfortable for him or her and appropriate for the person's mate. Here are two illustrations—one about asking for feedback, and another about offering it:

- "I felt a little awkward at the party last night. Did you notice any blunders on my part, or could you recommend how I might have handled that sensitive issue with Sally better?"
- "Well, I don't know that I would label this a 'blunder,' but it did seem that you spent almost the entire evening in one corner, while others were waiting to talk with you. As for your interaction with Sally, she might have been less defensive had you pulled her into the other room alone before discussing something so personal."

Practice New Behaviors on One Another

Some ways couples wish to grow may require significant changes in their behavior. Developing new behaviors requires practice. We can work on some behavioral changes on our own, but for others, our progress will be best if we practice with someone else—in this case, our spouse. To succeed in this endeavor:

- Decide on specific (not general) changes you wish to make.
- Focus on one of these behaviors to practice first. (You can try more later, after succeeding with one.)
- Let your mate know when you're going to try it out. (Surprises don't work well in this case.)
- Depending on what it is you want to practice, consider:
    —Observing as your mate models the behavior first, before trying it out yourself.
    —Role-playing the desired behavior as you interact together.
    —Doing a "role-reversal" to see it from your mate's perspective.

A young man wanted to eliminate his habit of using crude language with his wife when he was angry. To do this, he and his wife picked a time when all was calm. First, he wrote a brief list of phrases to express his strong feelings without being disrespectful, then the two of them practiced a couple of different scenarios using role-playing. After a few such role-playing sessions, they both reported that he had been able to vent his frustrations during a tense moment without swearing!

Focus on Complementarity

No person can possibly be superior at everything. Each of us has some things we're better at and others we're not so good at. In a thriving marriage, partners don't spend time putting one another down for the many ways each is deficient. Instead, they concentrate their energies on determining how each can use their personal strengths to help compensate for the other's weaknesses.

This is the essence of "complementarity." As a couple, take stock of all the strengths, special abilities, and positive qualities each of you is blessed with. Consider the sum total of these as your joint reservoir—your "pool of positives" either mate can draw upon. When it appears that one mate's weaknesses are creating a problem in the marriage, consider if it would be dealt with best by offsetting it with a strength of the other spouse.

> 🌿 *Consider the sum total of both partners' personal strengths as a "pool of positives" either mate can draw upon.* 🌿

Suppose one of you is a somewhat meticulous perfectionist, while the other is likely to overlook many details but is good at getting things done quickly. Rather than harping on each other for the ways this particular weakness can cause problems, why not figure out how you can capitalize on each other's strengths to your mutual benefit?

*S*USAN:

Tres and I have very different strengths and weaknesses. Recently, we undertook a major project which made many of these very clear to both of us. We decided to build a "designer bathroom" to be part of an extended master bedroom. We could have hired the work to be done by others, but we wanted to take this on ourselves for a variety of reasons—not the least of which was to have the satisfaction of learning and stretching in some very different ways. This project enabled us to discover how we could work together in a manner that our differences would help us get the job done better.

Tres is great in theory and vision, and also good at paying attention to the tiniest details; in some things he can be the ultimate perfectionist—which I admit can sometimes drive me nuts! But, he's not so hot when it comes to the mechanical or technical side of life: Programming a VCR is his form of "nightmare!" In technical things, he almost needs to be led by the hand, but he is willing to follow instructions from someone else who knows what to do. I'm the mechanical one in our marriage and can at least read a set of instructions without getting bogged down. On the other hand, I can't hammer a nail straight to save my life. I like to move right along and get things done, while he can be more of a plodder.

At any rate, this is how we used our differences in ways that were complementary to each other: Tres worked and reworked the plans to come up with a rather elegant "designer bathroom." (Actually, we both enjoy the designing part, and I must say, many of the special touches were my own!) When it came to much of the necessary "grunt" work on the project, I told him what to do, and he did it. I was in charge of figuring out how to do the electrical wiring. The textured ceiling—which basically called for someone skilled in working rapidly—was primarily my job. Many tasks we simply worked at side by side, where-as others were taken on by one or the other of us, depending on how much time we had available.

It would have been easy for me to become resentful that my husband did not have the know-how to build the bathroom; of course, all of the other men in our neighborhood could do it (at least that's what I thought!). Instead, I came to appreciate his strengths of vision, meticulous attention to detail, and his desire to learn how to do the hard physical labor I was incapable of. He relied on my confidence and skill in technical aspects, my ability to do things quickly, and my insistence on moving things along. What we both came to realize is that neither of us could do it alone; we needed each other to complete the project. By working together, we not only derived great satisfaction from undertaking and completing a difficult challenge together, we wound up learning a great deal about ourselves and our varied strengths.

Because of me, we moved the project forward continually. Because of Tres—who has an amazing capacity to push himself, and many nights stayed up almost all night—the bathroom was completed in a way that pleased both of us. That doesn't mean it was easy or without frustration. But, instead of arguing about whose way was "best," we kept our vision focused on what we both wanted, and acknowledged that we needed each other—largely because of our differences—and moved forward to reach our goal.

It's very natural for couples to pay attention to and be bothered by each other's flaws. It's not as natural—but much more productive—to concentrate on the cumulative assets in our marriage's own unique "pool of positives." By drawing from this rich reservoir of resources, we can do a better job of filling in each other's "gaps." Couples who take this approach are practicing a much neglected but highly beneficial type of spousal synergy. This is one habit that helps both spouses really feel like they're in a thriving relationship.

Become Creative Catalysts

In chemical terms, a catalyst is an agent that enhances the chemical reactions between other chemical compounds. In marriage, husbands and wives can act like catalysts to bring out the best in each other and maximize their growth as a couple. Partners in a thriving marriage recognize the value of enhancing the creative processes they can bring to bear. Creativity, in any form, reinforces a couple's sense of vibrancy in their relationship. Ultimately, then, a husband and wife need to do all they can to catalyze their creative interaction.

How can they do this? One of the simplest ways is by brainstorming more often. Couples can brainstorm to come up with new shared experiences, solve problems, and enhance their growth and development in other ways. For example, what if the two of you have decided you want to pursue goals that would be considered extremely ambitious under the best of circumstances? The problem is, your situation is anything but ideal, so in order to succeed will require some very fancy footwork, indeed. Nevertheless, you are both convinced you can do it and are committed to do whatever it takes to realize your dream. What's called for, however, is a strategy that will enable you to take the tough, necessary steps.

This is where brainstorming comes in. If both spouses focus their creative energies on coming up with the solution, they will find the answer. Millions know, from their own personal experiences, that seemingly impossible obstacles can be overcome 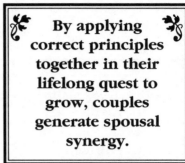 when they adopt the mind-set of "possibility thinkers"—then doggedly stay focused on the task until they find a way to "make it happen." Impossible dreams come true all the time for those who persistently pursue them. Paraplegics learn how to ski with the patient encouragement of their companions; couples who have been financially devastated can rise together from destitution to prosperity; partners who come from a long history of abusive relationships can learn to cultivate wonderful marriages.

Here's the exciting reality: What works for one person works even better for two. The power that's unleashed from a committed couple is far more than double what is possible for one person on his or her own. In fact, the yield from such a joint cooperative effort sustained over time is magnified many times over the combined output of two individuals working separately. This is how a husband and wife generate spousal synergy—by applying correct principles together in their lifelong quest to grow.

Nurture Joy Forever

Some husbands and wives are not content to be merely life partners; they want to be eternal partners. (This is especially true for those couples who actually succeed in creating a little bit of "heaven on earth" in their marriage.) Many of us know husbands and wives whose bonds of love seem to grow closer and closer over the years. Such couples are not necessarily commonplace—but neither are they rare. A man and woman such as this feel so connected, they just love being around one another! Some husbands and wives develop such unity and love for each other based on decades of cultivating a true oneness of heart and mind, they even come to look more and more alike in their physical appearance.

> ❧ **Any couple hoping** ❧
> **to nurture joy**
> **forever must learn**
> **to cultivate a**
> **thriving**
> **relationship in**
> **their ongoing**
> **daily interactions.**

These are true soulmates who would love their relationship to go on forever. And why wouldn't they? Wouldn't any man and woman, whose relationship just keeps getting better and better, want their love for each other to be never-ending? Millions are convinced that even after they die, their relationship can persist in the eternities, and that the two of them can actually have their own "forever family." For such persons, nurturing marriage forever is more than simply a generalized longing to always stay connected; they firmly believe that they can be.

There's a real difference, however, between saying we believe something and demonstrating our beliefs by our actions. Any couple who would ever hope to somehow live together forever recognizes that they must learn to live together very well in their daily interactions with one another. A blessing as marvelous as this would surely require a willingness to do whatever it takes on the part of both husband and wife. Those who would nurture joy in their marriage forever must learn to cultivate a thriving relationship over time; day in and day out, year after year. It's not a single goal they can pursue and succeed in nor a destination to arrive at. Rather, to nurture their marriage forever is an ongoing process couples must persist in as they travel together throughout life.

In some ways, it doesn't matter if a couple believes they can extend their relationship with one another beyond the grave. For those who are convinced this can be, they also know that the kind of relationship they develop now, in their mortal lives, will directly influence what kind of relationship they might share in heaven. Therefore, it's clearly in their best interest to do all in their power to cultivate a great marriage each day—throughout their entire lives. For those who don't necessarily believe their relationship could ever continue beyond the grave, it still serves their marriage best to act as though this were the case. Doing what it takes to "nurture a marriage forever," in reality, means making every day together a wonderful one.

Ultimately, the couples in both cases win where it counts: in the quality of the life they share together, day in and day out. In either case, they have created for themselves a heaven on earth by ensuring that their most impor-

> **All couples who learn to *Grow* together can take their relationship to a much higher level.**

tant relationship in life is, in fact, a thriving one. Besides, who knows? Even the couples who don't have any conviction about life after death might be pleasantly surprised to find their "heaven on earth" can become a heaven in heaven, after all!

With couples in either case, the implication is the same. These are people who really want to apply the *Grow* practice. They want to become all they can be—in their personal development and as marriage partners. And they recognize that the best way to do this is to draw upon the help available from their chosen companion, beloved soulmate, supportive helpmate, and life/eternal partner, and to be equally committed to bringing out the best in their mates. Husbands and wives who do this experience great joy in their lives.

Whatever your beliefs or hopes about the longevity of your relationship or "life after life," we strongly encourage you to take your relationship to a higher level by learning how to *Grow* together. Besides, any traveler is more likely to enjoy the companionship of his or her partner when both partners are growing.

MAIN IDEAS:
Grow

- Married persons need a "we" orientation instead of a "me" focus.
- A couple's shared vision consists of the unifying mutual goals they establish.
- Spousal synergy is the process partners use to achieve their goals.

The guidelines to developing a shared vision are:
- Develop a Marital Mission Statement.
- Begin where you are.
- Consider "times and seasons."
- Analyze and prioritize.
- Establish goals and objectives.

The ways to enhance spousal synergy are:
- Be effective as sounding boards.
- Take advantage of invaluable feedback.
- Practice new behaviors on one another.
- Focus on complementarity.
- Become creative catalysts.
- Experience joy as you seek to *Grow* together and bring out the best in one another.

20 QUESTIONS
to Ponder and Discuss

First, ask yourself the following questions about how you and your life partner are doing in your efforts to grow. Then discuss these questions with your life partner by asking: "How am I doing?" and "How might we improve?"

1. Are we aware that without a unity of purpose and direction in our relationship, our marriage is most likely to become stagnant, wither, and eventually die? Do we realize the benefits we'll gain by developing a shared vision?

2. Have the two of you discussed your personal philosophies of life—your core beliefs and values—to determine how they can be integrated into a joint Marital Mission Statement?

3. Do you focus your energies on growing forward, beginning where you are and building upon any previous progress?

4. Have you carefully considered and discussed where each of you are in terms of the times and seasons of your lives?

5. What plans have you made to evaluate your growth as individuals and as a couple on a regular basis?

6. When you take stock of your challenges and progress, do you make adjustments that will help you meet your changing needs?

7. In developing a sense of shared vision, have the two of you determined which aspects of your vision call for "dreams to work for" (goals), and which are "specific objectives" you've committed to achieve by a certain time?

8. In planning for your growth, have you established goals and objectives? Have you done this both as individuals and as a couple? Can you name them?

9. Have you analyzed each of your objectives to determine which ones might be best achieved by preparing a more detailed action plan to follow up?

10. Considering all the ways you want to grow, have you prioritized where each objective fits within the framework of all other responsibilities and goals that are important in your life?

11. To what extent do you consider your spouse to be your chosen companion, best friend, soulmate, helpmate, and life partner? What can the two of you do to make this even more so now than it may have been previously?

12. How can you apply the concept of spousal synergy more effectively as husband and wife?

13. Do you feel comfortable approaching your mate to help you think aloud and sort through various issues to formulate ideas or solve problems? Are there ways to improve this?

14. Are each of you clear about communicating to one another when what you really want is a "listening ear"? Are there ways you could be an even better sounding board to your mate?

15. Do you both feel secure enough, personally and in your relationship, to freely elicit and take advantage of feedback from one another? How could this be improved to your mutual benefit?

16. Are there any behaviors or habits you'd like to change that could benefit from role-playing or practicing with your spouse?

17. Have you taken inventory of your combined personal strengths and viewed them as a "positive pool" you can draw upon to support one another in personal challenge areas and fill in each other's gaps?

18. Are there ways the two of you could replace the habit of focusing on one another's personal deficiencies with the habit of complementarity, seeking ways to combine your strengths more effectively?

19. How can the two of you use brainstorming and being "possibility thinkers" to unleash the power of becoming creative catalysts for one another? Are there other things you can do to increase your joint productive output?

20. What else have you learned about the *Grow* practice (outside of this book) that you can apply to your benefit?

Now What?

After evaluating where you are in this practice, use the *KISS Marriage Maker*™ to identify goals and actions to improve those areas which need help. You might want to concentrate on one area at a time for a week or two, and then move on to another area. This could be an effective way to specifically improve and see the results of your efforts.

GROW:
Ideas to Consider

The following list of ideas may be a place to start as you determine specific things you will do to grow in shared vision and spousal synergy with your life partner:

- Tell your spouse about your ultimate "dream" in life—what you would like to accomplish or experience if you had no limits whatsoever.
- Complete this four-part exercise on personal growth.
  - A. Consider where you are in your personal growth in the following facets of balance: physical, social, emotional, mental, temporal, and spiritual.
  - B. Write at least one goal or objective for any areas where you'd most like to improve.
  - C. Share these with each other.
  - D. Discuss how you might assist each other.
- Make a brief list of core beliefs and values that matter the most to you as an individual.
- Share these with your mate.
- Express a simplified version of your "philosophy of life" with one another.
- Discuss your thoughts on how you want your lives to be different as a result of being married.
- Discuss how you might combine some of your most important beliefs, values, philosophies of life, and marital goals into a Marital Mission Statement.
- On a personal level, reflect on where you've been and where you're headed in terms of the times and seasons of your life as an individual. Discuss this with each other while considering the past, present, and future seasons in your relationship with one another.
- Reflect upon and discuss your marriage expectations for one another.

- Together, determine some goals and objectives that you'd like to pursue together.
- Write down any shared goals and marital objectives you've decided upon. Be sure that for any marital objectives where it is appropriate, you establish action plans to help you follow through and achieve them.
- Make it a point to prioritize your goals and objectives in writing. This may help prevent you from getting bogged down or overwhelmed with a comprehensive plan that could be unrealistic or unwise.
- Evaluate your growth as individuals and as a couple on a regular basis: once or twice a year, on your anniversary, or monthly, as you prefer.
- On an occasion when you need to sort through a problematic issue, or need a listening ear, ask your mate to be your sounding board.
- Make the opportunity to ask your life partner for feedback about something you want to improve.
- Select an area where you want to improve. Ask your mate if he or she would be willing to join with you in role-playing the new behavior, model it for you, or let you practice it together in some other way.
- Do this three-part exercise to strengthen the complementarity in your marriage:
  A. Each of you complete a "strength inventory" of your personal, positive qualities.
  B. Consider the sum of the strengths on both lists as a "positive pool."
  C. Discuss how you might draw upon this joint resource listed in your "positive pool."
- Brainstorm to consider how you can accomplish a worthwhile but difficult goal. Ensure that you both approach brainstorming with the attitude of being "possibility thinkers."

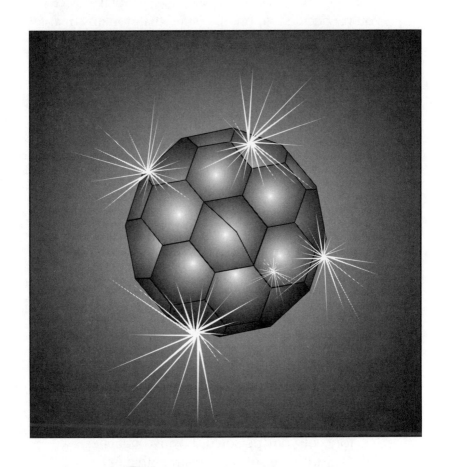

Thriving Marriage

A FORK IN THE ROAD . . .

Choose Which Path
You Will Follow

$\mathcal{W}$ELL, you've made it down the road this far. To all those who cared enough to have read this book—newlyweds and seasoned veterans alike—we hope you've found the reading worth your while. No matter what your purpose may have been in reading this book—having a wonderful trek, discovering a better way to travel, experiencing more joy, getting it "right" this time, or moving beyond your doubts—if *Enjoy the Journey Along Your Marriage Highway* has proven helpful to the two of you, then the two of us will feel very gratified.

You're now at a very important fork in the road of your current or potential marriage. The road now splits into three distinct paths you could choose to follow. The first road is a tragic way to travel; the second one can sometimes prove quite worthwhile, and the third one offers an incredible journey.

The first path is the path of least resistance, the way of the copout. This is the road of married persons who do nothing to make their marriage any better. It could be because they've tried before and nothing has worked, they've been hurt before, or they're simply lazy couch potatoes when it comes to exerting any efforts—even those in their own behalf. A lack of knowledge about what to do is a reason for some, but not one for anyone who has read this book. Here are three of the common reasons people don't change or grow:

- "I've paid my dues." These folks feel they've already worked on their marriage before, and it's just not right that they should have to put any more into it.
- "Nobody's perfect." Although this is, of course, true for every one of us—married or not—we shouldn't use this weak cop-out as an excuse to do nothing at all.
- "Analysis paralysis." There's a real paradox in this variety of non-growth. People get so caught up in analyzing their relationship, they don't focus on actually changing or helping themselves, or their partners, to progress.

ℰRES:

As a professional counselor, I have always found it puzzling that many therapists place so much emphasis on analyzing people and their relationships in great detail. Frankly, there's no end to the ways human beings and their problems can be explored and examined. It's quite possible to develop a deep understanding and extensive insights about who has done what to whom, why they've done it, and what the results are of all these "whys" and "wherefores." Nevertheless, it seems to me what really matters is determining what people can do about their lives and relationships so they can progress and grow. Maybe that's why I never saw myself as a "shrink," but rather viewed my role as that of an "expander."

My recommendation for those seeking help from any mental health professional is to request that the therapist spend less time "shrinking" them (analyzing their problems and issues) and more time "expanding" them (helping them grow through solving their challenges and realizing their potential). This is just as true for those in marriage counseling as it is for those in individual therapy.

Regardless of the reason they choose this route, couples who stay on the no-growth road are bound to get stuck in lots of ruts all along the way.

If this book goes on your bookshelf, and whatever ideas you've gleaned from reading it get filed away somewhere in your mind, you will be taking the well-beaten second path chosen by the majority of those who read books. Glean what you can from what you've read. Hopefully, the main ideas and some of the interesting examples or key phrases will come to mind once in a while. In this way, you and your partner will benefit from this exposure, and your relationship will be better than it otherwise would have been. If the book thus serves to help you and your spouse in any way at all, we, as authors, will be delighted.

Three Paths at the Fork in the Road:

1. **Copout; do nothing.**
2. **Develop interesting insights; gain bookshelf knowledge.**
3. **Continually nurture a thriving relationship.**

Then there is a third path, the "road less traveled" by most people who are exposed to a new resource. Once such travelers become convinced that a certain path is one that will lead them to a place they really want to go, they are eager to use the road to pursue a chosen quest. Those who are unwilling to simply survive their spouse, and don't want to settle for a mediocre marriage but want a truly thriving relationship with their life partner, know this is no simple task. A single reading of a good book—no matter how good—just won't cut it.

A thriving marriage is impossible to achieve by any shortcut or "quick fix" solutions. Rather, a relationship this special calls for a lifetime commitment to continually nurture it—which is why some opt for the third path. Travelers who choose this road do not feel they must devote untold hours to making their marriage great. Most are extremely busy and have lots of other things to occupy their time, but the quality of their marriage is something such persons value highly. They don't consider the core relationship in their life something they can take for granted. Instead, they make it a point to continually care for their marriage. They nurture this relationship on an ongoing basis, just as they do their health, their children, and their careers.

Throughout the book, we've encouraged readers to get the most out of this resource by taking the time to ponder and discuss the *20 Questions* and to review the *Ideas to Consider* included at the end of each chapter. If you have not yet done so, now would be a good time to go back and actually do these exercises. They are intended to help you better understand and use the *Six Vital Practices* so you can achieve a thriving marriage with your partner. This can be done chapter by chapter, a little at a time.

We also suggest that you learn about and use the *KISS Marriage Maker*™ tool described in *Appendix A* and *Appendix B*. In many respects, the little *KISS Marriage Maker*™ is even more important than the ideas covered in the book itself, because it offers you a simple and convenient way to follow through in applying this information in your own marriage, where it will do you the most good.

Couples who choose to follow this third path will take full advantage of *Enjoy the Journey Along Your Marriage Highway*. They'll use it as a "Handbook for Marriage Travelers" to which they'll refer to help their journey go better. They will also make it a point to use the *KISS Marriage Maker*™ frequently—not out of a sense of duty or to complete some assignment, but rather because it serves their own purposes well, especially as a practical way to ensure that with their busy lives, they make time to make their marriage what they want it to be.

As we've mentioned before, please remember this: Use your own discretion in determining how you'll use anything we've shared with you. Figure out what makes sense and what doesn't. Apply ideas in whatever way works best for you. Do so at your own pace; the Road of Marriage is not a road race. Every couple will have their own goals and styles in traveling their own paths. The last thing we would want is for a husband and wife to begin on the third path, then abandon it altogether and settle for the first road because they felt so overwhelmed with what they saw as unrealistic or excessively demanding. There is only one expectation: Do the best you can. Sometimes your best efforts will be extensive, and other times you won't do a thing. That's all right. Whether you decide upon and follow through with many different goals each week or work on only a single application for an entire month, it's okay. What matters is that you do something to help your marriage become better.

When both of you sincerely strive to use these resources in the way they were intended, they will help you. A person who consistently applies correct principles eventually reaps the rewards. This is also true for husbands and wives working

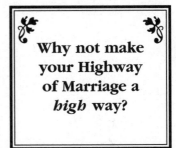

Why not make your Highway of Marriage a *high* way?

together to make their marriage all that it can be. We believe this can be a blessing for the two of you. We wish you much happiness and joy along your way!

As long as you're on the Highway of Marriage, why not make it a *high* way? After all, this is the best possible way to ensure that both of you Enjoy the Journey!

APPENDIX A

KISS Marriage Maker™ Tool

$\mathscr{C}\!\mathscr{A}\!\mathscr{T}$ THE end of each chapter, we have encouraged couples to use the *KISS Marriage Maker*™ tool to ensure that they actually apply the *Vital Practices* to improve their marriage. Its size and design make it very convenient to use and it fits readily into whatever time management or personal planner you might use. (See the example on the following page.)

K.I.S.S.*
Marriage Maker™
(Keep It Simple Sweetheart)

Weekly Applications of
The 6 Practices for Thriving Relationships

1. Review Practices	4. Schedule Applications
2. Target Needs	5. Implement Plans
3. Establish Goals	6. Evaluate Progress

Date:_____

Goal:
_____
_____
_____

Goal:
_____
_____
_____

Goal:
_____
_____
_____

Goal:
_____
_____
_____

Goal:
_____
_____
_____

Goal:
_____
_____
_____

Thriving Marriage

Follow these simple instructions (summarized at the top of each weekly *KISS Marriage Maker*™ form):

1. Review Practices

How do you feel about your marriage right now? You may wish to consider different ideas you've learned as you've read the entire book, or perhaps recall your answer to just one of the *20 Questions* toward the end of any given chapter.

2. Target Needs

Decide which facets of your marriage you'd like to concentrate on this week. Some individuals may wish to focus on several aspects of all six practices; others may prefer to work on only one.

3. Establish Goals

Briefly write these down on a *KISS Marriage Maker*™ form.

4. Schedule Applications

Determine when you will apply your goals; if necessary, schedule a time to do so, coordinating with your mate.

5. Implement Plans

Carry out whatever plans you've set for the week.

6. Evaluate Progress

Evaluate how well your plan worked out, determine if you'd like to modify your plan next time, or if you're ready to move on to another practice.

To give you an idea of different ways you can use this tool, we have included three examples. In the first illustration, the wife has written two goals, and the husband has written one. In the second, the man has identified two weekly applications of a *practice,* and the woman has selected one. In the third example, each partner has decided to work on six separate applications during the week—one per day for each of the six practices.

K.I.S.S.*
Marriage Maker™
(Keep It Simple Sweetheart)

Weekly Applications of
The 6 Practices for Thriving Relationships

1. Review Practices	4. Schedule Applications
2. Target Needs	5. Implement Plans
3. Establish Goals	6. Evaluate Progress

Date: *4/13 – 4/19*

Goal:
• Go to the park after supper and, while we're swinging, share some of our favorite childhood memories.

Goal:
• Let Kevin know that I'm willing to support him in the way he disciplines Sally, even though I personally prefer to handle her tantrums differently.

Goal:

Goal:

Goal:

 Thriving Marriage

K.I.S.S.*
Marriage Maker™
(Keep It Simple Sweetheart)

Weekly Applications of
The 6 Practices for Thriving Relationships

1. Review Practices	4. Schedule Applications
2. Target Needs	5. Implement Plans
3. Establish Goals	6. Evaluate Progress

Date: Week of April 13

Goal:
• Make it a point to ask Mary to tell me about one challenge and one good insight she's had during her day.

Goal:

Goal:

Goal:

Goal:

 Thriving Marriage

K.I.S.S.*
Marriage Maker™
*(Keep It Simple Sweetheart)

Weekly Applications of
The 6 Practices for Thriving Relationships

1. Review Practices	4. Schedule Applications
2. Target Needs	5. Implement Plans
3. Establish Goals	6. Evaluate Progress

Date: Week of 8/24

Goal:
  • Talk with Linda about how my campaign speech fiasco in 8th grade still makes me scared when I'm in front of groups.

Goal:
  • Ask Linda if she would work with me for a few weeks while I practice my presentation to the committee on 9/17.

Goal:

Goal:

Goal:

Goal:

Thriving Marriage

K.I.S.S.*
Marriage Maker™
*(Keep It Simple Sweetheart)

Weekly Applications of
The 6 Practices for Thriving Relationships

1. Review Practices	4. Schedule Applications
2. Target Needs	5. Implement Plans
3. Establish Goals	6. Evaluate Progress

Date: August 24 – 30

Goal:
  • Be more aware of timing in bringing up sensitive issues. Ask Sam permission to share a concern with him after dinner.

Goal:

Goal:

Goal:

Goal:

Thriving Marriage

K.I.S.S.*
ᴏ𝓜𝐚rriage ᴏ𝓜𝐚ker™
(Keep It Simple Sweetheart)

Weekly Applications of
The 6 Practices for Thriving Relationships

1. Review Practices   4. Schedule Applications
2. Target Needs   5. Implement Plans
3. Establish Goals   6. Evaluate Progress

Date: _Week of October 26_

Goal:
• *Talk with Jim about the two of us taking up country dancing together.*

Goal:
• *Focus on treating Jim with the respect and dignity he deserves. (Watch my tone of voice and language I use when we're with others.)*

Goal:
• *Tell Jim just before we make love some night that I'd like to try slowing things way down. Find romantic music with a slow rhythm.*

Goal:
• *Begin a discussion about our expectations for one another. Be sure to include our feelings about relating to those of the opposite sex.*

Goal:
• *Make a list of the ways the differences between us have made our marriage better. Tell Jim my thoughts and ask for his ideas.*

Goal:
• *Ask Jim to tell me what he really thinks about the way I act when his kids are here. Have him suggest how I can improve.*

 𝓣hriving ᴏ𝓜arriage

K.I.S.S.*
ᴏ𝓜𝐚rriage ᴏ𝓜𝐚ker™
(Keep It Simple Sweetheart)

Weekly Applications of
The 6 Practices for Thriving Relationships

1. Review Practices   4. Schedule Applications
2. Target Needs   5. Implement Plans
3. Establish Goals   6. Evaluate Progress

Date: October 26 - November 1

Goal:
• Monday: Prepare dinner and clean up food. Wash and dry dishes together with Amanda while we listen to music.

Goal:
• Tuesday: Tell the guys at lunch 3 things I really like about Amanda (besides her great body!)

Goal:
• Wednesday: Give Amanda a gigantic hug when I leave in the morning and first thing after I walk in the door.

Goal:
• Thursday: Talk to Amanda about my resentment over her folks, but be sure to calm down first so I don't lose my temper.

Goal:
• Friday: Make sure we do something Amanda wants that night, asking her to go camping with me next weekend.

Goal:
• Saturday: Take a couple of hours to begin talking about how we can work things out so I can start taking classes at college.

 𝓣hriving ᴏ𝓜arriage

Remember, there's no "right" way to use the *KISS Marriage Maker*™; whatever works for you and your partner is best. For example, some marriage partners prefer to determine their application ideas individually, while others find it's best to make decisions and plans about applying the *Six Practices* together. Nevertheless, couples who want to maximize the benefits of a thriving marriage for themselves generally try to establish the habit of doing something specific on a weekly basis.

Be patient with yourself and your mate. It may take several weeks of experimenting to figure out how this tool can best serve your own needs and circumstances. It takes persistent effort, day in and day out, year after year, to make your marriage all that you want it to be.

We're convinced that you will both be well rewarded for your efforts. After all, having a wonderful relationship with your beloved companion can bring an immense joy into your life that's hard to come by in any other way. We wish you every success in using *Enjoy the Journey Along Your Marriage Highway* and the *KISS Marriage Maker*™ tool to make your marriage the satisfying and enduring relationship it was meant to be!

We want every couple to have their own set of *KISS Marriage Maker*™ tools, so we'll give you a complementary set of 26—13 blue and 13 pink (his and hers)—enough for both partners to use for three full months. To obtain your free *KISS Marriage Maker*™ tools, or to order additional copies, see *Appendix C.*

APPENDIX B

"Jump-Start" Your Marriage in Six Weeks!
(Six Weeks to a Thriving Marriage)

 $\mathscr{T}$HE KEY to making any change in our lives is to apply useful information. In the case of *The Six Vital Practices for a Thriving Marriage*, you need to:

- Take the information you've read in the pages.
- Filter it through your own mind.
- Put it into practice in your own life.

This isn't always easy. We all know a lot of good things we can do, but we don't always do them. The *KISS Marriage Maker*™ was designed as a simple tool to help you apply what you've learned on a weekly basis. This appendix contains some suggested guidelines for three different approaches you might take to implement information from *The Six Vital Practices for a Thriving Marriage*. By using your selected method, in combination with the *KISS Marriage Maker*™ tool, in just six weeks you'll be well on your way to making your marriage much more of what you'd like it to be!

There are many approaches you could use. We've outlined three methods you might want to consider as you develop your own plan; no single method is best. They are different to accommodate the differing needs, styles, and desires of married people. You may find that one of these methods is well-suited for the unique time constraints or special challenges in your relationship, or perhaps you'll come up with your own variation that works even better. What matters is that you and your partner decide upon and follow through with some plan to put into practice what you've learned on a regular basis.

A Few Ideas to Keep in Mind

Read the *Beginnings* chapter first. It contains very important information to help you get the most from *Enjoy the Journey Along Your Marriage Highway*. Avoid the tendency to jump immediately "head-first" into whatever practice you find most problematic. It's usually best to achieve some successes in easier areas before tackling the tougher challenges in your relationship. If you implement either Method 1 or Method 2, you'll have an initial exposure to all six practices during your first six weeks. Then you can go back and spend more time focusing on whichever practices you'd like. During your first few weeks and months, concentrate on the practices that will do your marriage the most good. Make sure that both of you continue to apply all six practices so that your relationship remains a thriving one.

Add, drop, create, or modify any application goals used in your weekly habit of developing and nurturing a thriving marriage by using the *KISS Marriage Maker*™ tool. Periodically, go back to the *20 Questions* sections at the end of each chapter and ask yourselves how you're doing. Remember to use question number 20 frequently, as this is an ongoing opportunity for both of you to determine how you can continually synthesize and integrate different ideas into making your marriage what you'd like it to be. Developing a thriving marriage can be challenging, but overall, this process ought to bring both of you much satisfaction. Remember, your purpose is to experience greater joy in life together, so be sure to have fun along the way!

In today's busy world, it can be a real challenge to find time to spend on improving your marriage relationship. Nevertheless, those who are committed and creative will undoubtedly find a way to nurture this most important of all relationships. And remember, only those who make the effort to invest in their relationship—even when this requires some sacrifice—can hope to reap the rewards and enjoy the benefits of a thriving marriage!

Method 1: **"One at a Time"**

Focus on one separate practice each week. This is an easier, slower-paced, and more gradual approach than the others. In this method you'll work on one practice at a time during the course of the entire week, then move on to the next practice during the next week. Follow these steps:

1. Schedule a specific time to read the book together (or at least a time you can discuss it together).
2. Read one chapter a week, and answer and discuss the questions at the end of the chapter.
3. Select ways each of you will apply the practice during the coming week (writing your goals on your *KISS Marriage Maker*™ tools to ensure follow-through).
4. At the end of the week, move on to the next practice until you have completed the book.
5. If you'd like to, go back and work on any specific area of challenge you may have.
6. Continue to establish at least one weekly application goal for one of the *Six Practices* for the rest of your life!

Method 2: **"Expanding Effort and Energy"**

Start with *Share*, then add one new practice each week. In this method you begin with a single practice, then gradually build upon your previous efforts by introducing one additional practice each week. So, by the end of six weeks, you're applying all six practices at the same time. Follow these steps:

1. Schedule a specific time to read the book together (or at least a time you can discuss it together).
2. Start with *Share* and read one chapter a week; then answer and discuss the questions at the end of the chapter.
3. Select ways each of you will apply the practice during the coming week (writing your goals on the *KISS Marriage Maker*™ tools to ensure follow-through).

4. At the end of the week, read the next chapter on *Care* and set goals for both practices during the second week.

5. Continue adding a practice each week until, at the end of six weeks, you're applying and setting goals in all six practices.

6. Continue to set weekly application goals in all *Six Practices* for the rest of your life!

Method 3: "As You Like It"

Focus efforts on practices randomly, according to need. This approach is especially well-suited for husbands and wives whose learning styles, circumstances, or personal preferences call for significant flexibility. Couples using this method should remember to begin their efforts in an area where they are likely to experience successful results.

1. Schedule a specific time to read the book together (or at least a time you can discuss it together).

2. After reading *Beginnings*, scan the rest of the book, and select the practice you'd like to start with first. (You may choose it because it's the easiest, most interesting, very timely, or sounds like the most fun.)

3. Select ways you will apply the practice during the coming week (each of you writing your goals on your individual *KISS Marriage Maker*™ tools to ensure follow-through).

4. At the end of the week, continue focusing your efforts on the same practice, or select and read another chapter and set goals for that practice.

5. Continue learning about and applying each practice until you've covered all six.

6. Continue to set at least one weekly application goal related to the *Six Practices* for the rest of your life!

APPENDIX C

Additional Resources

Share This Unique Book with Others

Wouldn't it be nice to travel the Marriage Highway with others who are also focused on nurturing thriving relationships? Whether you buy it for yourself, or as a gift to family, friends, or newlyweds, this treasured volume is certain to enrich any couple.

Code 2420 hardcover ....**$ 23.95**

A Handy Tool to Make It Work Weekly

Order a FREE 3-month supply of *KISS Marriage Makers*™. You'll then want to order a one-year supply. This includes 104 *KISS Marriage Makers*™—enough so both you and your partner can each have your own set of these easy-to-use tools for every week of the year!

- **Code 261X:** ....**No Charge**
  (Complimentary 3-month supply for couple)
- **Code 2610:** ....**$ 4.95**
  (1-year supply for couple/104, color-coded)

*This book is also available at your favorite bookstore, or call **Toll Free 1-888-932-6266** for Visa or MasterCard orders. Prices do not include shipping and handling. Your response code is EJMH.*

If you feel *Enjoy the Journey Along Your Marriage Highway* is a worthwhile resource for your marriage, you'll love a parent-involvement resource we developed!

The **School Success System**™ is for highly committed parents, grandparents, and educators. This audio learning program centers around *Helping Kids Succeed in School*, a six-hour audiocassette series—perfect for today's busy adults.

This resource features a national team of contributing authors who teach you how to foster a love of learning in your child, develop an effective school-home partnership with your educators, and apply specific strategies to provide the kind of support most essential for each developmental stage of your child's life—all the way through college! The contributing authors include Jack Canfield (co-author of the national, bestselling *Chicken Soup for the Soul* series), several state teachers of the year, and seasoned parents.

It also comes with a *Guidebook*, which provides a detailed, written summary of the entire audiotape series and a *Personal Education Action Plan* to help you apply what you've learned in a customized education "game plan" for your own child. It has been acclaimed by parents, educators, and PTA leaders nationwide. The **School Success System**™ includes a six-cassette album, a 65-page illustrated *Guidebook*, and a convenient *Personal Education Action Plan*.

Code 3420 (complete set) ....$ 79.95

If you found *Enjoy the Journey Along Your Marriage Highway* to be a worthwhile source of valuable ideas, we have good news for you:

Live Presentations & Counseling

Couples who want to learn how they can apply the ideas in this book to their own relationship can attend a live presentation. Seminars, retreats, and other marriage enhancement programs are also available. These can either be with Tres and Susan in a joint presentation, or with Dr. Tanner doing the presentations alone.

For further information about scheduling Dr. Tanner for a keynote, seminar, or training session custom-tailored for your organization, or to schedule Tres and Susan for a joint presentation, please contact:

Home/Work®—The Family Connection®
Consulting Services
15721 Bernardo Heights Pkwy., Suite E-410
San Diego, CA 92128

Phone: 1-888-44-FAMILY (1-888-443-2645)
Fax: (619) 675-7504

For inquiries about professional counseling call:

1-888-77-CONNECT (1-888-772-6663)

About the Authors

TRES and SUSAN TANNER are striving for a thriving relationship as best friends, soulmates, and life partners. Together they conduct retreats, seminars, workshops, and lectures for couples and families. They collaborated in developing the **School Success System**™ audio learning program, a parent involvement resource featuring a national team of 23 contributing authors. Among their greatest joys in life are their children and grandchildren.

Tres Tanner is a family relations and personal development specialist, a professional counselor and speaker, and founder of Home/Work®—The Family Connection®. For over 25 years, Tres has been speaking and counseling on marriage, parenting, and personal development throughout North and South America. He has taught at several major universities and has served as associate professor and department chairman. He received a masters degree in Marriage, Family & Child Counseling from Chapman University and, in 1975, earned a Ph.D. in Family Relations at Florida State University, where he was a university fellow.

Susan Tanner has been a health care professional for over 15 years working in hospital administration and managing several specialty clinics. She has been an adjunct professor of health care marketing at Weber State University, where she also served as chair of the curriculum review committee for the Health Administrative Services program. After graduating magna cum laude, she earned a masters degree at Utah State University.

Tres and Susan live and work in San Diego, California.